Forever Yours

Wedding Quilts, Clothing & Keepsakes

AMY BARICKMAN

Project Instructions
Margaret F. Cox

C&T PUBLISHING

Editor: Liz Aneloski
Technical Editor: Joyce Engels Lytle
Copy Editor: Judith Moretz
Cover Designers: Diane Pedersen, John Cram and Micaela Miranda Carr
Design Director: Diane Pedersen
Book Designer: Micaela Miranda Carr
Illustrators: Richard Sheppard, Lorelei Brede, Alan McCorkle, Jay Richards
Photographers: Tracy Thompson and Gary Rhoman, unless otherwise noted
Cover and Quilt Photographer: Sharon Risedorph

Library of Congress Cataloging-in-Publication Data

Barickman, Amy
     Forever yours : wedding quilts, clothing & keepsakes / Amy Barickman: project instructions by Margaret Cox.
     p.   cm.
     Includes index.
     ISBN 1-57120-042-8
     1. Handicraft.   2. Weddings—Equipment and supplies
     3. Wedding decorations.   4. Gifts.   I. Title
     TT149.B37   1998
     745.594'1—dc21   97-37164
                             CIP

Printed in Hong Kong
10 9 8 7 6 5 4 3 2 1

Dedication

To my mother
and grandmother,
who inspired me by their
encouragement and examples.

Creativity is not
inherited, but learned
and matured.

Contents

Preface

The intent of *Forever Yours: Wedding Quilts, Clothing & Keepsakes* is two-fold. First, we hope anyone planning a wedding, bride-to-be, mother of the bride, or professional wedding coordinator, will be inspired to create lasting memories and a personalized wedding event. Second, we share the many unique and beautiful projects and quilts with others who cherish handmade things and hope they too will want to make the projects for pleasure and gift giving. We realize that most of us are novices who want to achieve a hand-crafted, yet professional, look. To this end we offer thorough, easy to follow step-by-step instructions, complete patterns, and helpful illustrations. With over fifty projects in the book, there is something for the novice and the long-time sewer or crafter alike. Personal choices and color schemes can also be incorporated into any of the projects to truly reflect individual style and meaning. Our goal is to help you make your special day one of love, happiness, and unforgettable experiences.

Introduction

Personalizing the Wedding of Your Dreams . . .

A beautiful wedding is one of life's eventful moments. Most women anticipate the romance and elegance of their own wedding day from childhood. There is something significant about experiencing a personalized wedding. Carrying out plans to reflect the interests and relationships that are especially meaningful to you may seem like a true challenge. The intent of this book is to remove some of the intimidation and inspire you to create gifts, decorations, and clothing with vintage romantic style tailored to your own personal needs. When you incorporate thoughtfulness, meaning, tradition, and love into your wedding, family and friends will share in your unforgettable moment forever.

The projects for this book came together as a lifelong love of handmade workmanship and old things became a personal expression in the theme and design of my own wedding. The unique styling of my wedding dress, with a hand-pieced crazy quilt bodice, is a prime example of "something old, something new." Fabrics taken from my mother's wedding gown were designed into the modern styling of the dress bodice. Other projects in the book are just as personal and meaningful: treasured dolls and teddy bears dressed in wedding frills for a whimsical bridesmaid's gathering, romantic wedding accents and accessories, a silk ribbon embroidered trousseau, and a collection of heirloom quilts.

The collaboration of several talented designers (including my mother) truly produced an heirloom collection of meaningful handmade wedding projects and made this book possible. Throughout the book we have provided projects for the beginner as well as the experienced crafter. Many projects, like the romantic vintage necklace purses or the floral wedding wreaths, are simple to create and require minimal materials. We have made every effort to produce simple, yet thorough instructions to encourage you to make as many projects as possible. Also, an illustrated reference section provides the how-to for the stitches and techniques used throughout the book. Along the way hints on how to make the projects fit your personal needs, as well as ideas for incorporating vintage laces, trims, and fabrics into your own wedding treasures are presented. I am thrilled to share my wedding experience and the lovely projects that resulted. Finally I invite you to include something vintage into your own wonderful wedding day.

A Word About Vintage . . .

No doubt you have heard the adage "everything old is new again." Most of the projects in this book rely on renewed sentimental romance of the past: romance found in vintage baubles, tapestries, velvets, and lace remnants and romance discovered in family traditions, treasured keepsakes, and faded photographs. At the same time, projects in this book successfully meld the old with the new to mark the most important occasion uniting two people together.

Creating a vintage-theme wedding is easier than you think. Begin by rummaging through a family attic for heirlooms and inspiration. Old family photographs, especially a grandparent's wedding picture, can be used to create a sense of tradition. Photocopies of the photograph can be used on ceremony programs and invitations, or can be framed and displayed creatively among centerpieces at the rehearsal dinner or reception.

Visit local antique stores or flea markets to discover endless supplies of old laces and luxurious fabrics. Do not be discouraged if an heirloom piece or flea market find has a stain, wear, or damage. Be creative and use other laces, beads, or baubles to cover up the flaws and show off the good parts in elegant accessories and decorations. Masking with beautiful silk ribbon embroidery is another clever method for disguising the less-than-pretty spots. Another vintage trick is to make new materials look antique. To give a new piece vintage appeal, consider using tea to dye laces, ribbons, and fabrics (see instructions, page 114). Also, use elements from old costume jewelry to give a project that antique charm.

An old family wedding photograph links past to present as the circle of love continues.

You may not have to go farther back than a childhood experience to find a keepsake that really captures your sentiment. For instance, a priceless self-portrait colored by the bride as a child is a lighthearted presentation to mark the bride's long-dreamed-about wedding. We enlarged and transferred a childhood "work of art" onto a T-shirt. Rummage through your own keepsakes to rediscover childhood pictures, or have the young attendants in your wedding color a picture to capture the blissful day. There are products on the market for transferring artwork to fabric, but a professional T-shirt shop can also do the job. The masterpiece can also be reduced and photocopied onto card stock to make the bride's personal one-of-a-kind thank you notes.

Child's play makes a T-shirt and bridal stationery unique and unforgettable.

Finally, a wedding with a vintage and handmade theme is all about finding meaningful keepsakes and traditions that can be functional as well as beautiful. Remember, it is your wedding, so have fun with it!

Details,
Details...

*Silk ribbon embroidery and lace make wedding
accessories something special.*

Accents For Romance

Details that make a wedding memorable are the simple yet elegant one-of-a-kind accents. Adding vintage romantic laces, trims, and silk ribbon embroidery to ordinary accessories makes them something special. In this section you will find beautifully embellished framed keepsakes, fabric-covered boxes, and decorative accents that are easy to make as treasured gifts or functional accessories for the wedding day.

Design placement

Brocade Picture Frame
Designed by Donna Martin

(Photo page 8)

INSTRUCTIONS

1. Refer to the illustration and follow Silk Ribbon Embroidery (page 115) to stitch pink spider web roses and green lazy daisy leaves on each lace appliqué.
   Glue pearls to the appliqués.

2. Inserting pearl sprays under each appliqué, glue the appliqués and pearl sprays to corners of frame.

SUPPLIES
Brocade fabric-covered frame
Two lace appliqués for frame
  corners
4mm pink silk ribbon
4mm green silk ribbon
Pink perle cotton thread
Assorted pearls
7 pearl sprays
Craft glue

Heart Keepsake Box
Designed by Donna Martin

(Photo page 8)

INSTRUCTIONS

Refer to the illustration above and follow Silk Ribbon Embroidery (page 115) to stitch pink spider web roses and green lazy daisy leaves on the lace appliqué. Glue pearls onto the appliqué and glue the appliqué to the lid of the box.

SUPPLIES
Fabric covered heart-shaped box
Lace appliqué to fit lid
4mm pink silk ribbon
4mm green silk ribbon
Pink perle cotton thread
Assorted pearls
Craft glue

Lacy Garter
Designed by Donna Martin

(Photo page 8)

INSTRUCTIONS

1. Weave 3mm pink ribbon through the center of the lace. Knot and trim the ribbon ends.

2. Cut the elastic length in half. Working on the wrong side of the lace and pulling the elastic to fit the lace, place the elastic lengths $3/8$" apart at center of lace and use a zigzag stitch to sew over the elastic lengths. Secure the elastic ends.

3. Sew the lace ends together to form a circle.

4. Refer to illustration for Brocade Picture Frame (page 9) for stitches on the appliqué and follow Silk Ribbon Embroidery (page 115) to stitch variegated ribbon spider web roses and green perle cotton lazy daisy leaves on the lace appliqué.

5. Sew the appliqué to the garter.

> As an alternative to making a garter, embellish a purchased garter with laces and beautiful silk ribbon embroidery, or add small ribbon roses, silk flowers, and pearl sprays to the garter. To make the garter look antique, tea dye it before embellishing (follow Tea Dying, page 114).

SUPPLIES

- $2/3$ yard $2^1/4$" double-edged lace
- 2" x $2^1/2$" lace appliqué
- $2/3$ yard elastic cord or narrow elastic
- 1 yard 3mm pink silk ribbon
- 1 yard 4mm pink-and-yellow variegated silk ribbon
- Green perle cotton thread

An elegant gilded frame and memorable fabrics make a treasured keepsake.

Framed Crazy Quilt
Designed by Sandy Belt

A beautiful framed crazy quilt captures the finery of fabrics and splendor of the wedding in a simple display. The treasure can be easily transformed into a gilded vanity tray by covering the handmade quilt with glass. We used the same vintage fabrics found in our quilted wedding dress bodice (page 27). However, any combination of wedding fabrics can be pieced to create a unique bridal heirloom. Or fill your frame with a quilt piece discovered among grandmother's keepsakes or found at an antique shop. Embellish the quilt with additional accents—elegant stitches, antique buttons, a vintage brooch, or even golden wedding rings.

INSTRUCTIONS

1. Cut a piece of muslin for quilt backing, 3" larger than the frame.

2. Use silk fabrics and muslin backing and follow Crazy Patch Block (page 113) to piece a quilt large enough to fill the frame.

3. Using three strands of floss, embroider decorative stitches along each seam of the quilt. (We used herringbone, feather, buttonhole, fly, and chevron stitches, pages 114 and 115).

4. Sew laces and buttons to the quilt. Sew pearls in clusters of three to the quilt.

5. For ribbon embellishment, follow Silk Ribbon Embroidery: French Knot Couching (page 118) to anchor ribbon to the quilt, and twirling and looping ribbon for design.

6. Trim the quilt to fit the frame. Secure the quilt into the frame.

SUPPLIES

½ yard muslin
Ivory silk fabrics
1 yard 4mm ivory silk ribbon
Embroidery floss
Assorted laces, buttons, and pearls
9½" x 12" gold oval frame

Heirloom Box
Designed by Ninette Gehle

Vintage laces and linens can bring old-fashioned charm to wedding accessories and keepsakes.

INSTRUCTIONS

1. Cut a vintage lace piece slightly smaller than the lid; round the corners of lace.

2. Sew the vintage lace piece to the lid. Sew lace trim along the edges of vintage lace, and the small motifs to each back corner of the lid.

3. Measure around box and add ½"; cut a length of flat lace this measurement. Press under ¼" on each end to the wrong side. Sew flat lace around box close to bottom edge, meeting the pressed ends at center back.

4. Sew heart beads to the front corners of the lid.

5. To embellish flat buttons, sew seed beads on the top of each button. Sew flat and shank buttons along the lace trim on the lid.

6. For each ribbon flower, use pink ribbon and follow Making Ribbon Flowers and Leaves: Fuchsia (page 121) to make six fuchsias.

SUPPLIES

8" x 3½" x 4" fabric-covered treasure box
Vintage lace for lid
⅝ yard ¾" lace trim and 2 small lace motifs for lid
⅔ yard 1" flat lace for box
Small flat and shank pearl buttons
Assorted clear seed, round, and crystal beads
2 pearl heart beads
½ yard 1¼" pink silk ribbon
⅔ yard 7mm green silk ribbon
18 small yellow stamens

7. For fuchsia streamers, thread a large needle with an 8" length of green ribbon. Knot the ribbon end opposite the needle. Insert the needle into the top of one fuchsia and out the bottom of the flower. Carefully pull the ribbon until the knot rests inside the bottom of the flower. Insert the same needle and ribbon into the bottom of a second fuchsia and pull it out at the top of the flower. Unthread the needle and knot the ribbon end. Carefully pull the ribbon back into the second fuchsia until the knot rests inside the bottom of the flower. Repeat to make two more fuchsia streamers.

8. Hold the streamers together and fold in half. Knot folded ends of the streamers. Sew the streamers to the lid. Sew desired beads to the knot of the streamers.

Potpourri Basket *Designed by Ninette Gehle*

(Photo page 11)

SUPPLIES

Half circle cut from a 10" diameter vintage linen
Half circle same size as above cut from green fabric
2/3 yard 1/4" flat lace trim
1 yard 1/4" light green ribbon
1/2 yard 1½" pink-and-green variegated silk ribbon
1/4 yard 7mm dark green ribbon
Assorted small buttons, pearls, and gold charms

INSTRUCTIONS

1. For the lining, roll the outer edge of the green fabric half circle to the wrong side to enclose the raw edge; hand sew in place.

2. Fold the lining into a cone shape, matching the right sides and straight edges. Sew a 1/4" seam along the straight edges. Repeat for the linen half circle.

3. Turn the linen cone to the right side. Place the lining into the linen cone and tack along the top edges to secure.

4. For each handle, cut one 12" length from each light green ribbon and lace trim. Place one ribbon and one lace length together, fold the ends to one side, and sew the ends to the top front of the linen cone; repeat to sew a handle to top back of cone. Tie remaining light green ribbon into a bow around the center of the handles.

5. Tie the dark green ribbon into three small bows. For each ribbon flower follow Making Ribbon Flowers and Leaves: Fuchsia (page 121) to make six ribbon fuchsias from the variegated ribbon.

6. Sew fuchsia flowers and bows to the basket; sew a button or bead on top of the bow. Sew additional charms to the basket as desired.

To transform a new linen into a vintage look-alike, tea dye the fabric following the instructions (page 114). It's as good as old.

A satin-covered folder with lace and ribbon detailing creates an elegant accessory for the bride's personal correspondence.

Bride's Stationery Folder

Designed by Margaret Cox

INSTRUCTIONS

1. For the folder, place the brocade fabric wrong side up and place the flap and front and back cover mat board pieces on fabric about 1/4" apart. Trim away each fabric corner and fold the fabric over the outer corners of the flap and front cover piece; glue in place. Fold and glue the fabric over the edges of the flap and both cover pieces.

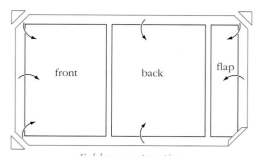

Folder construction

2. Cut a piece of satin slightly smaller than the folder for the inside. Center and glue the satin to the inside of the folder, covering the brocade fabric edges.

3. On the outside of the cover, glue the 1" bridal lace trim along the edge of the folder front, wrapping the ends to the inside. Glue the 3/4" lace trim along the inside edges of the folder, covering the raw edges of the satin and bridal lace trim ends.

4. Cut pieces of satin 1" larger than each remaining inside front and back mat board pieces. Cover each piece with satin, gluing the raw edges to the back as in Step 1.

SUPPLIES

11" x 15½" ivory satin brocade fabric for folder cover
Approximately ⅜ yard ivory satin for inside folder
1½ yards ¾" lace trim
⅓ yard 1" bridal lace trim
2 lace appliqués
⅝ yard ¼" diameter rayon twisted cord
1 yard of ½" ivory sheer ribbon
3mm mauve silk ribbon
3mm green silk ribbon
4mm pink, purple, and yellow variegated silk ribbon
Purple perle cotton thread
Assorted round and iris pearls, sequins, and seed beads
Small adhesive hook and loop circle
Drawing compass
Craft glue
The following pieces cut from white mat board:
    1½" x 10" for flap
    7" x 10" for back of cover
    5½" x 10" for front of cover
    6¾" x 9¾" for inside front
    5¼" x 9¾" for inside back
    1" diameter circle

Japanese Ribbon Stitch
yellow, pink, and green

French Knots
mauve and purple

Lazy Daisy Stitch
green

Loop Stitch
pink

Spider Web Rose
purple

Pearl

5. Cut a 2" length from the sheer ribbon. Cut the remaining sheer ribbon into four equal lengths. For the pen holder, fold the 2" ribbon length in half and glue the ends to the wrong side of the back satin-covered piece at the left edge. Place one ribbon length diagonally across each bottom corner of the front satin-covered piece; glue the ends to the underside. Place another ribbon length diagonally across the opposite top and bottom corners of the back satin-covered piece; glue the ends to underside.

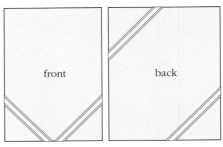

front   back

Ribbon placement

6. Center and glue the satin-covered inside front and back pieces to the inside of the folder about ¼" apart.

7. Referring to the illustration below as a guide, follow Silk Ribbon Embroidery (page 115) to stitch designs on lace appliqués. Sew pearls, beads, and sequins to the laces.

8. Glue appliqués to the front of the folder.

9. For the closure, glue satin to one side of the mat board circle; trim the fabric edges even with the circle. Coil and glue the twisted cord onto the uncovered side of circle, tucking the raw ends of the cord under at center and to back at end.

10. Extending half of closure over the edge of the flap, glue the satin side of the closure to the center edge of the flap. Adhere the hook circle to the satin side of the extended part of the closure. Adhere the loop to the center edge of the front of the folder under the closure.

Stitch placement

Bride's Portfolio

Designed by
Margaret Cox

Bride's stationery folder and portfolio for organizing correspondence. See cover photo.

INSTRUCTIONS

1. If necessary, cut the self-flap off of the portfolio along the top back edge and discard.

2. Cut two fabric pieces ½" larger on all sides than the front of the portfolio.

3. Referring to the previous illustration, follow Silk Ribbon Embroidery (page 115) to stitch the designs on the lace appliqués. Sew pearls, beads, and sequins to the laces.

4. Arrange the appliqués and doily on the right side of one fabric piece about 1" from the fabric edges. Sew the laces in place, leaving the outside edges unsewn to allow the trim to be placed under the lace later. Sew the button and additional pearls, beads, and sequins to the fabric.

5. Center the embellished fabric piece on the front of the portfolio, matching the bottom raw edge of the fabric to the bottom edge of the portfolio; glue in place. Fold and glue the top fabric edge to the inside of the portfolio. Fold the fabric over the side edges and glue in place. Repeat to glue the remaining fabric piece to the portfolio back.

6. Starting at the center top and mitering the corners, glue the trim along the edges of the front and back of the folder. Sew the edges of the laces over the trim.

7. For tassel ties, apply a bead of glue 11" from one end of the chair tie and another bead of glue 12½" from the opposite end of the chair tie; allow to dry. Cut the chair tie at both glued areas, setting aside the left-over twisted cord (about 8").

8. Glue the end of the shorter tassel tie to the center front of the folder over trim ends. Glue the remaining tassel tie to the center back. Gluing the cord first to prevent raveling, cut 8" of twisted cord in half. Tucking the cord ends to the back, coil and glue one cord length into a circle over the ends of the front tassel tie; repeat for the back. Tie the tassel ties together at the front of the folder.

SUPPLIES

10" x 15" expandable pocket portfolio

Ivory satin brocade fabric for cover front and back of portfolio

Fusible interfacing (if needed)

3½ yards ⅝" ivory decorative trim

Ivory twisted cord chair tie with 3¼" tassels

2 lace appliqués and one small doily

3mm dark mauve silk ribbon

3mm green silk ribbon

7mm pink, purple, and yellow variegated silk ribbon

Purple perle cotton thread

Assorted pearls, beads, sequins, and one small button

Craft glue

Note: If color of the portfolio will show through the fabric, fuse interfacing to the wrong side of the fabric before cutting for project.

Inspired by the Victorian age, this unique box holds sewing necessities and is an elegant vanity accent.

SUPPLIES

12" square of ivory brocade satin for box

1/4 yard ivory satin for inside of box

Satin and silk scraps for lid

5" square of muslin

Polyester fleece

Low-loft polyester batting

Ivory embroidery floss

6" of 3/4" vintage flat lace for inside straps

1/2 yard ivory bridal lace trim

3/8 yard ivory rayon twisted cord

Assorted buttons, round and iris pearls, and seed beads

The following pieces cut from white mat board:

    4 1/4" square for lid

    2 1/4" square for bottom inside of box

    Four 2 1/4" x 4" rectangles for box sides

    Four 2" x 3 1/2" rectangles for inside of box

Art knife and straight-edged ruler

Transparent tape

Sewing items to fill the box

Craft glue

Bride's Sewing Kit
Designed by Margaret Cox

INSTRUCTIONS

1. For the outside of the box, refer to the illustration to cut out 4 1/2" squares from the corners of the brocade fabric square. Trim each corner of the remaining fabric shape.

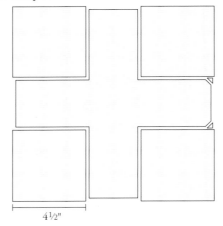

4 1/2"

Cut squares from the corners

2. Trim one 4 1/2" brocade square to a 3" square. Cover the 2 1/4" mat board square with the 3" fabric square, wrapping and gluing the corners, then the sides to the back.

3. Cut four 1" x 2 1/4" strips from another 4 1/2" brocade square. Center and glue one fabric strip over the ends (bottoms) of each large mat board rectangle.

4. Place the outside box fabric shape wrong side up. Arrange the fabric-covered square at the center of the fabric shape and larger rectangles around the square, leaving a small gap (the width of mat board) between the square and the rectangles. Glue the fabric-covered square in place.

Slash the inner corners of the box fabric shape to just within the center square.

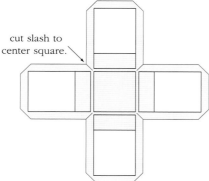

cut slash to center square.

Arrange the mat board pieces on the wrong side of outside box fabric shape

5. Glue the wrong side of the bottom edges of the rectangles to the wrong side of the outside box fabric shape. Fold and glue the fabric corners over the rectangle corners. Fold and glue the sides over the edges of the rectangles.

6. For the inside of the box, cut four rectangles of satin ¹⁄₂" larger on all sides than the remaining small rectangles. Cut two fleece and two batting pieces the same size as the small rectangles. Glue one fleece, then one batting piece, to one rectangle; repeat for a second rectangle. Cover all four rectangles with satin, pulling the fabric taut and wrapping and gluing the corners, then the sides, to the back of the rectangles.

7. Cut the flat lace in half for the inside straps. Center one strap horizontally on each unpadded rectangle; wrap and glue the ends to the back.

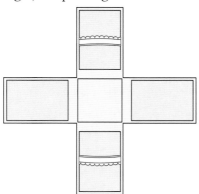

Center lace horizontally

8. Gluing the padded rectangles on opposite sides, center and glue the covered rectangles to the inside of the box.

9. For the lid, use a utility knife to score the square ³⁄₄" from each edge. Cut away the corner squares where the scoring intersects.

10. Fold the sides of the lid down and tape the corners together.

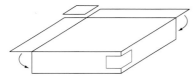

Fold sides down and tape corners

11. Cut a 2¾" square of satin. Center and glue the satin to the inside of the lid, smoothing the edges onto the sides.

12. For the top of the lid, follow Crazy Patch Block (page 113) using the satin and silk fabrics and 5" muslin square. Embellish the pieced quilt with desired embroidery stitches, buttons, pearls, and beads.

13. Cut a piece of fleece the same size as the top of the lid; glue to the top of the lid. Center and glue the quilt piece to the top of the lid, smoothing the edges over the sides and the corners of the lid. If necessary, trim the corners to eliminate bulk.

14. Cut a 1½" x 12" strip of satin. Starting in the middle of one side of the lid (front) and matching one long edge of the strip to the top edge of the lid, glue the strip around the sides of the lid, overlapping the ends at the front. Wrap and glue the edges of the fabric to the inside of the lid, smoothing the fabric at the sides and corners as you go.

15. Starting at the center front, glue bridal lace trim around the sides of the lid; trim. Glue twisted cord along the top edge of the lace. Use a running stitch to gather the straight edge of the remaining bridal lace trim into a circle. Sew the lace circle to the lid, covering the cord and lace ends.

16. String several pearls and beads onto a threaded needle for 1", securing the last bead by stringing a seed bead and passing the needle back through the previous beads. Sew the bead dangle to the center of the lace circle. Repeat for a second dangle and a 3" dangle folded in half to form a loop. Sew a button to the center of the lace circle.

Ribbon Floral Garter *Designed by Margaret Cox*

(Photo page 16)

SUPPLIES

1⅓ yards 1½" ivory wired
  sheer ribbon
1⅛ yards 1" ombré ivory wired
  satin ribbon
⅔ yard of ⅜" ivory picot-
  edged satin ribbon
⅓ yard ¼" elastic
Thread to match ribbons
Pearl stamens for loop petal
  flower

INSTRUCTIONS

1. Cut a ⅔ yard length from the sheer ribbon.

2. Center picot-edged ribbon on the sheer ribbon. Sew close to each edge of the picot-edged ribbon to form a casing.

3. Insert the elastic through the casing; secure the elastic ends and adjust the ribbon gathers.

4. Bring the ends of the ribbon together and sew ¼" from ends.

5. For ribbon flowers and leaves, follow Making Ribbon Flowers and Leaves: Loop Petal Flower, Crushed Rose, and Gathered Leaf (pages 118-119 and 122) to make one loop petal flower and two leaves from the ombré ribbon and two crushed rose buds from the remaining sheer ribbon. Sew the flowers and the leaves to the right side of the garter covering the seam.

Quilted Heart Cushion

Designed by Ninette Gehle

INSTRUCTIONS

1. Trace the heart pattern onto tracing paper; cut out.

2. Cut one heart from each quilt and fabric square.

3. Matching the right sides and straight edge of the trim to the outer edge of the heart, baste lace trim to the quilt heart.

4. Using a ¼" seam allowance, sew the hearts right sides together, leaving an opening for turning. Clip curves, turn to right side, and press.

5. Stuff the cushion with fiber fill. Sew the opening closed.

6. For the hanger, knot each end of the ribbon length about 1" from the end. Fold the ribbon in half and knot about 3" from the fold to form a loop. Knot again 1½" from the first knot.

7. Sew the lace motif to the top of the pillow. Sew the hanger to the lace motif.

8. For a bead dangle, string three to four pink beads, one heart bead, and one seed bead onto a threaded needle. Insert the needle back through the beads to secure. Sew the bead dangle to the pillow below the hanger. Repeat for a second dangle.

A sweet and old-fashioned heart cushion makes a nice gift for attendants, or it can be used as a ring bearer's pillow.

SUPPLIES

7" square cut from a vintage quilt
7" square of fabric for back
Polyester fiber fill
½ yard of ½" lace trim
Small lace motif
⅔ yard of ¼" pink ribbon
2 pearl heart beads
Assorted seed and pink beads
Tracing paper

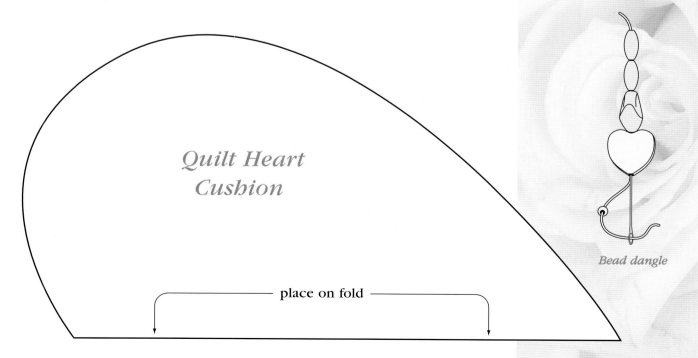

Quilt Heart Cushion

place on fold

Bead dangle

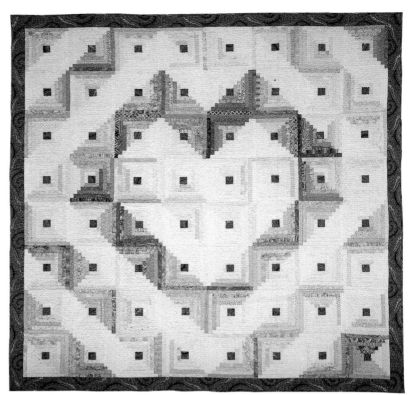

Log Cabin Quilt in Neutrals, Carolie A. Hensley, machine quilted by T F & E of Pittsburg, CA, 104" X 104", sixty-four 12" finished Log Cabin blocks.

Log Cabin Quilt in Neutrals

Note from the designer, Carolie A. Hensley:

This Log Cabin quilt was designed for my son Todd and daughter-in-law Jennifer as a wedding gift. Jennifer likes neutral colors and approved the color scheme not knowing the quilt was to be for them.

Selecting fabrics for a scrap Log Cabin quilt is a lot of fun. I chose to use a neutral color scheme, but this quilt will be beautiful in any color scheme you choose. My quilt contains over one hundred different fabrics. None of the fabrics is used more than once. Every block is different; no two are alike. The colors are graduated to give the effect of a light side and a dark side on each block. Choose a focal print fabric for the center square of each block and the border, pulling other neutral colors to blend. You will need white on white prints, white on muslin prints, natural prints, beige, and golds. Use both warm and cool colors. Be sure to include plaids, stripes, florals; any print fabric that fits your color scheme. No solids were used. Buy as many fabrics as you can afford; more is better. Be sure to purchase 100% cotton fabrics of good quality from your nearest quilt store.

FABRIC TIPS: Fabrics should be pre-washed in warm water, no detergent, dried in the dryer, and pressed. Dark colors should be watched for running. If a fabric runs, use Retayne™ to control the bleeding. If the fabric will not stop bleeding, throw it away.

INSTRUCTIONS

CUTTING

Cut two strips parallel to the selvage for the center squares, then cut the strips into sixty-four 2½" x 2½" center squares.

Cut two 1½" x 42" strips from each piece of log fabric. Set the remaining fabric aside until needed. If you spend all your time cutting, you will never be sewing!

BLOCK ASSEMBLY

A Log Cabin block is usually pieced with the colors graduating from the center block outward on each of the four sides. Only the color values change to create your light and dark sides. Each log is a different fabric. Arrange your fabric strips so you can pull the lightest colored strip to sew onto the center block. All seams are constructed with a ¼" seam allowance.

1. To sew one Log Cabin block begin with the center square A (2½" x 2½"). With right sides together, sew strip B to square A.

Sew B to A

2. First press the seam with a shot of steam while flat, then press toward strip B. Trim the edge even with the center square A.

Press and trim

3. Choose strip C and place it right sides together with AB unit. Sew across the pieces. Press flat and then press toward strip C. Trim edge even with the center square.

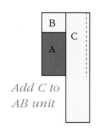 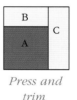

Add C to AB unit   *Press and trim*

4. Next, sew D to AC side of ABC unit. Press flat and then toward strip D. Trim the edge even with the AB side.

5. Continue sewing, pressing, and trimming until the block is completed (five logs on each side of the block). Always sew in a clockwise direction.

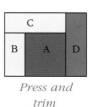

Add D to ABC unit   *Press and trim*

6. Continue sewing until 64 blocks are completed.

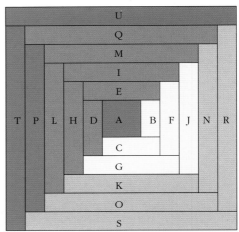

Log Cabin block

QUILT ASSEMBLY

7. When you have completed the blocks, now is the time to arrange the design of the blocks. Lay your blocks out on a table, floor, or design wall and arrange into a heart or other configuration you decide is pleasing. It may take a few days to decide which blocks should be where.

8. When you finally like the arrangement, mark the upper left-hand corner of each block with masking tape: Block 1, Row 1; Block 2, Row 1; Block 3, Row 1 until you have marked each block and each row. Believe me, if you don't mark your blocks you will turn a block around and will have to rip it out and start over. If you mark the block corners, you will be less likely to make a mistake! Remember, your seam ripper is your best friend!

9. Sew the blocks together, starting with Row 1, and sew Block 1 to Block 2, Block 3 to 4, Block 5 to 6, and Block 7 to 8. Then sew these block pairs together to complete Row 1. Then sew Row 2. Press the seams to the left. Continue until all 8 rows are sewn. Alternate the pressing direction from one row to the next so the seams will lay flat when sewing the rows together.

10. When the entire top is together, look for mistakes or uneven seams. Should you need to correct anything, do it now. Then press the top completely. Stay stitch the entire outside edge ⅛" from the edge to keep the blocks from stretching.

BORDERS

11. Measure the width of the quilt across the middle. Cut two borders 4½" wide by the width of the quilt. Pin and sew the borders onto the top and bottom. If you have a walking foot for your machine, this is a good time to use it, as it will keep the fabrics from stretching.

12. Measure the length of the quilt across the middle. Cut two borders 4½" wide by the length of the quilt. Pin and sew the borders onto each side.

13. Press the quilt top well.

LAYERING

14. You are now ready to sandwich your quilt top, batting, and backing fabrics together to make the quilt. Be sure your backing and batting are at least 4" larger all around the quilt top. Cut and sew three 3¼ yard pieces together for the quilt backing. Spread the pieced back fabric, right side down, onto large tables or a hard floor. Tape the edges down with masking tape. Layer the batting on the backing fabric. Place the quilt top on top of the batting and backing, centering it. Now pin baste or hand baste the layers together. The basting should be about 3" apart; any larger and you may get puckers on the back. When you are finished basting, you can remove the tape and lift the quilt off the surface. You are ready to quilt. Now the fun begins!

QUILTING

15. Quilting your quilt is a personal decision. If you enjoy hand quilting, do it. Machine quilting done correctly is beautiful. If time is against you, hire someone who does good work and have it quilted.

BINDING

16. Cut four binding strips parallel to the selvage 2¼" wide by the length of the sides plus 3" to 4".

17. Sew the four strips together, making a long continuous strip. Fold in half lengthwise, right sides out, and press. At one end of the binding, fold the raw edge ¼" to the wrong side. Start sewing with this end 3" or 4" from the corner using a ⅜" seam. When you reach ⅜" from the corner, back tack and place needle down into the quilt and pivot the quilt. Lift the needle and fold the binding like a corner of a gift-wrapped package; start sewing ⅜" from the corner, back tacking after the first two or three stitches.

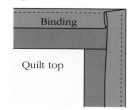

Back tack ⅜" from corner;
continue stitching ⅜" from corner.

18. Continue to the next corner. Repeat the process. This will give you mock mitered corners. Finish sewing the binding by overlapping the ends. Trim off the excess binding.

19. Turn to the back side and whip stitch the binding to complete the quilt.

This beautiful neutral quilt will match any new couple's home decor.

Dresses and Accessories

Elegant silks, laces, and fabrics create textures of romance and elegance for dresses and accessories with personal style.

Something Old, Something New

One of the most important decisions regarding the wedding day is what the bride and wedding party will wear. Many brides strive to achieve a balance between contemporary and traditional wedding styles. The challenge is to incorporate modern style with old-fashioned, yet endearing, wedding traditions. Romance and elegance are themes that never go out of style. Therefore, combining romantic textures of vintage fabrics and laces with today's fashion and accessories is an excellent solution to the traditional versus contemporary dilemma. From the crazy quilt bodice wedding dress, to the Victorian elegance of a lace and satin vest or romantic ribbon-adorned bridesmaid dresses, the dresses and projects in this section unite traditional needlecraft techniques with modern styles for a dramatic romantic effect.

A Mother's Wedding Account

One of a mother's dreams is to help plan her daughter's wedding. Actually, I had looked forward to this for many years. This anticipation probably stems from the wonderful creative experience my mother and I had thirty years before when I was organizing my own wedding.

When I was married in the mid-1960s, I had recently graduated from college with a home economics teaching degree. That summer I was working in a fabric store in Michigan where I had worked from the time I was a young girl. I had sewn most of my clothing and always knew someday I would design my wedding gown. I had even practiced on my antique dolls.

My dream gown evolved into a beautiful creation with silk and alençon lace. My mom embellished the dress with ten yards of seed pearls. I made my veil and there was lace for my shoes as well.

Amy's mother and father

Amy and her mother, Donna Martin

I designed and even made some of the bridesmaid's dresses using fabrics and laces from Stuarts Fabrics where I worked. The experiences from my handmade wedding are memories I have always cherished and traditions I hoped to carry on as a creative part of my daughter's wedding.

Amy's husband Bobby proposed to Amy at our family's Northern Michigan home in a most unique way—posting a banner in the woods stating, "Amy, Will You Marry Me!"

With the engagement announced, wedding plans began immediately. Although my life was very busy running two retail stores, I wanted to participate in my daughter's wedding rather than have the so called "luxury" of having her take over. Many of the ideas Amy and I created together were what helped make her wedding special and meaningful. Times were busy, but I would not trade the experience. Our gathering of family and friends was special to everyone.

Many brides wear their mother's or grandmother's wedding dress, but Amy was afforded the wonderful opportunity to have designers Patrick Lose and Lenny Houts design and make her gown. The stunning crazy quilt bodice melded Amy's selection of new embroidered silk with the recycled silk from my handmade wedding dress.

As the mother of the bride, I wanted to wear something simple, beautiful, and memorable. An elegant ensemble resulted, with a vest made using some of the same silks and clusters of lace from my wedding gown. I embellished the vest with antique pastel, variegated silk ribbon and pearls, and matched a tiered ruffled skirt for a complete romantic look. I made six bridesmaid's dresses, spending eight hours on each one, embellishing the necklines with ribbon rosebuds, silk ribbon embroidery, and seed pearls. The design was created by my good friend Kathy Pace, who originally designed the dress for her own daughter's trousseau.

To coordinate the entire event even further, we created wedding decorations and keepsakes using the same techniques, fabric, and laces from the dress. I had endless joy seeing the fabric recreated in the form of Victorian slide purses, a miniature bride doll dress, lovely frame and box accents, and many other fineries. Truly pretty in form, the items served their function well. The handmade theme of Amy's wedding allowed me to fulfill my motherhood dream and relive my own wedding day all over again. Happily, an endless supply of new memories was forged seeing Amy carry on the tradition, grown up and off to her new married life.

This unique wedding gown is made by piecing elegant vintage and new textured silks in crazy quilt fashion. Seed pearls and gathered piping details embellish the bodice.

Quilted Wedding Dress
Designed by Patrick Lose and Lenny Houts

INSTRUCTIONS

FITTING BODICE AND DETERMINING FINISHED LENGTH

1. Use the pattern to cut the bodice pieces from muslin to make a test bodice. Baste the seams of the muslin bodice together. Fit the bodice to the body, pinning areas that are gapping and cutting, or letting basting out in areas that are too tight (generally, the bodice should fit close to the body with minimal ease). Check position of bodice waistline for appropriate placement. Record adjustments of test bodice.

2. Measure from waistline to desired finished length of dress; record measurement.

3. Transfer fitting adjustments to actual bodice paper pattern, or trace new pattern pieces onto tissue paper to reflect necessary adjustments. (Make any

Wedding dress pattern with puffy sleeve (or follow instructions here to adapt sleeve pattern to puffy sleeve)

Fashion fabric(s) for dress and piping (We used a combination of new and old fabrics, including embroidered shantung silks and fabric from an heirloom wedding dress. Refer to pattern for yardage, allowing extra for pattern alterations and quilted bodice.)

Fabric(s) for lining and underlining and dress notions specified by pattern

Muslin for test bodice and quilted bodice backing

1/4" diameter cotton cording for piping along bodice and neck edges

Pearls

Tissue paper (optional)

waist adjustments to the skirt and any armhole or shoulder adjustments to the sleeve and bodice patterns if necessary.) Lengthen or shorten the skirt pattern to reflect the desired finished length of the dress.

PIECING CRAZY QUILT FOR BODICE

4. Cut muslin rectangles 3" larger on all sides than each bodice pattern piece. Follow Crazy Patch Block (page 113) and use scraps of fashion fabric(s) to piece the quilt on each muslin rectangle.

5. Sew pearls to each quilted rectangle.

MAKING PUFFY SLEEVES

Note: Follow instructions to adapt the original pattern to a puffy sleeve pattern, or use a pattern with puffy sleeves. We recommend making a muslin test sleeve using the new pattern before making sleeves from fashion fabric. After making the sleeves, follow Constructing Dress instructions to finish and attach the sleeves to the bodice.

6. To adapt the pattern, determine the desired finished length of the sleeve and the amount of fullness at the top and at the lower edge of the sleeve (start by adding 3" to the fullness and decrease or increase as necessary).

7. Cut the original pattern apart between the sleeve cap gathering marks.

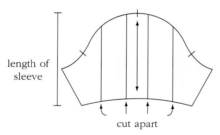

length of sleeve

cut apart

Cut pattern between marks.

8. Referring to the illustration, lay the sleeve pattern pieces right sides up on tissue paper, spreading out the pieces to create additional fullness (we allowed for more fullness at the bottom than at the top of our sleeve). Trace the outer edges of the pattern, adding extra length at the top cap of the sleeve and at the lower the edge of sleeve to create the "pouf" effect for the sleeve. Cut out the pattern.

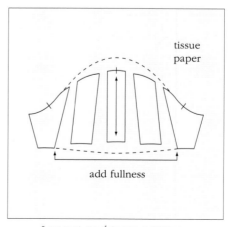

tissue paper

add fullness

Lay out and trace pattern.

9. Cut two sleeves each from fashion fabric and underlining fabric. For each sleeve binding, cut a 2" wide fashion fabric strip the same length as the finished bottom width of the sleeve plus 1¼". Press one long edge of each binding strip ¼" to wrong side.

10. Baste one sleeve and one underlining sleeve wrong sides together. Gather the sleeves at each sleeve cap between the gathering marks. Then gather the fullness of the lower edge of the sleeves, leaving approximately 3" of the underarm sections ungathered.

11. Match right sides and raw edges and use a ¼" seam to sew one binding strip to the lower edge of each sleeve. Press the strips over the raw edges to the back; sew in place along the folded edge of the strip.

CUTTING OUT AND CONSTRUCTING DRESS

12. Use the altered patterns and follow the pattern instructions to lay out and cut the skirt, sleeves (if needed), and other details from fashion, lining, and underlining fabrics. Cut each bodice pattern piece from the quilted rectangles.

13. Referring to the pattern instructions, sew the bodice pieces together. Sew the bodice lining pieces together.

14. To make piping, measure along neck, back, and lower edges of bodice; add 10". Cut a length of cording this measurement. Cut a 1½"-wide strip of fashion fabric twice as long as cording length (piecing as necessary). Place the cording on the center of the wrong side of the fabric strip; secure the end of the cording to the end of the fabric strip. Covering the cording, match the long edges of the fabric strip and use a zipper foot to sew close to the cording for about 6"; stop with the needle down in the fabric. Pull the cord to scrunch the fabric over the cord, behind foot; continue to sew and scrunch the fabric over the entire cord.

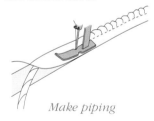

Make piping

15. On the right side of the fabric match the flange of the piping to the raw edges of the bodice and baste the piping along the neck, back, and lower edges of the bodice.

16. Sew the bodice lining to the bodice along the neck and back edges. Follow the pattern instructions to sew the skirt, sleeves, closure, and details, to attach the bodice, and to finish the dress.

Making your own veil is so easy and inexpensive. With a few simple elements and a little time a handmade veil can be a stunning bridal accent.

Beaded Headband Veil
Designed by Donna Martin and Amy

SUPPLIES

Silk linen fabric piece (or fabric to match wedding dress) to cover headband frame

Buttonhole twist thread to match fabric

Bridal buckram headband frame

1¼ yards 50" bridal illusion for veil

Elastic looping trim

2 clear hair combs

Pearls

Craft glue

INSTRUCTIONS

1. Trim the ends of the headband to fit just on top of the head.

2. Measure the width (from front to back) of the headband; multiply by 2 and add 1". Measure the length of the headband; multiply by 2 and add 3". Cut a piece of silk the determined width and length measurements.

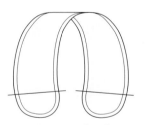

Trim ends of headband.

3. Matching the right sides and the long edges, fold the fabric piece in half and sew ½" from the long raw edges; turn to the right side.

4. Slip the headband into the fabric tube, scrunching and gathering the fabric over the headband. Center the tube seam on the underside of the headband.

5. With about 1½" of fabric extending past the ends of the headband, refer to the illustration below to fold the ends of the fabric to the underside of the headband. Sew the ends in place.

Fold ends to underside.

6. Sew a length of elastic looping trim to the underside of the headband about 1" from one edge.

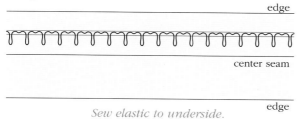

Sew elastic to underside.

7. Adjust gathers evenly and use buttonhole twist to sew from the front side to the back side through all thicknesses to secure the gathers on the headband. Glue pearls to the headband.

8. For the veil, fold the illusion in half lengthwise. Fold in half again from top to bottom. Refer to the illustration below to cut the curved edges of the veiling; unfold.

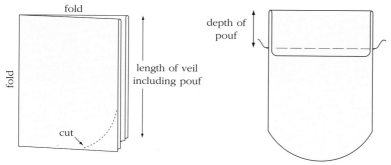

Fold in half twice and cut curved edges.   *Fold edge and gather.*

9. Referring to the illustration above, fold one end of the veiling (top) to the desired depth of pouf. Machine gather the veiling close to the raw edge.

10. Gather the veiling to fit the headband. Sew the gathered edge of the pouf and veil to the underside of the headband opposite the elastic looping trim. Glue additional beads to the pouf of the veil.

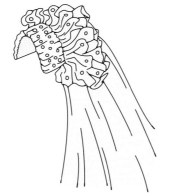

Sew gathered edge to headband.

11. Insert one comb into the elastic looping at each side of the headband.

*Romantic elegance abounds in these Victorian Slide Purses
decorated with lace, pearls, and silk ribbon embroidery.*

Victorian Slide Purse *Designed by Donna Martin*

INSTRUCTIONS

1. For inner bag, place bag and lining fabric pieces right sides together and sew ¼" seam along the long edges to form a tube. Press one end of the tube ¼" to wrong side. Turn the tube to the right side and press.

2. With the lining facing up, bring the ends to the center (center back of bag). Insert the raw end into the pressed end of the tube and slipstitch the ends together. Slipstitch the bottom of the inner bag together.

3. For the handle, find the center of the tieback cord. Wrap transparent tape around the center of the cord for about 1"; cut the cord in half at the center of the tape. Use ivory floss to wrap the cords of the handle together about 5" from the tassel end; knot and trim the floss. Sew the ends of the handle inside the top of the inner bag at each side.

4. To construct the outer bag, follow Steps 1 and 2, but do not sew the bottom of the bag together.

5. Using pink and green perle cotton and pink ribbon, stitch lazy daisy stitch leaves (page 114 and 117) and spider web roses (page 116) on the lace. Sew the embellished lace to the front of the bag with additional laces, pearl sprays, pearls, and sequins.

SUPPLIES

- Two 6½" x 11" ivory fabric pieces for inner bag and lining
- Two 8½" x 12½" ivory fabric pieces for outer bag and lining
- Assorted appliqué, doily, and motif laces (We used lace motifs cut from an heirloom wedding dress to coordinate with the bride's dress.)
- ⅓ yard each of ¾" flat and 3" bridal lace trims
- Pearl sprays
- Assorted pearls and sequins
- 4mm variegated pink silk ribbon
- Ivory embroidery floss
- Pink perle cotton thread
- Green perle cotton thread
- 18" ivory twisted cord drapery tieback with a 5" tassel
- Transparent tape

6. For the trim on the outer bag, sew narrow lace trim around the lower edge of the outer bag. Sew the wide lace trim to the inside of the bottom of the outer bag.

7. Slip the outer bag over the inner bag. Hand sew the top edges of the outer bag together between the handles.

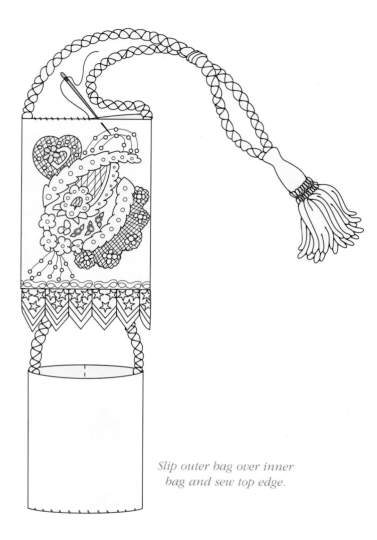

Slip outer bag over inner bag and sew top edge.

For in the dew of little things the
heart finds its morning and is
refreshed.

Kahlil Gibran.
The Prophet

SUPPLIES

Ivory dress with scoop neckline

4½ yards 1" sheer ivory wired
   ribbon

2 yards 1" ivory satin wired
   ribbon

3 yards 1" ombré ivory satin
   wired ribbon

Crinoline for ribbon flower
   backing (optional)

#10 and #11 sharps needles

Strong thread to match ribbons
   and dress

Silk pins

Pearl stamens and seed beads

Ribbon Flower Key

Crushed Rose
*three from sheer
ribbon*

Fuchsia
*four from sheer
ribbon, one from
satin ribbon*

**Large Flower with
Five Petals**
*three from satin
ribbon*

**Small Flower with
Five Petals**
*two from sheer
ribbon*

**Flower with Three
Petals, with stem
and calyx**
*three from satin rib-
bon, two from sheer
ribbon, stems and
calyxes from ombré
ribbon*

Gathered Leaf
*eight from ombré
ribbon*

*Romantic silk ribbon flowers create
a one-of-a-kind wedding dress.*

Elegant Ribbon Floral Wedding Dress
Designed by June Wildash Decker

INSTRUCTIONS

Refer to the illustration below and the Ribbon Flower Key and follow Making Ribbon Flowers and Leaves (pages 118–122) to make flowers, leaves, and stems from specified ribbons. Using the illustration as a guide, arrange flowers and leaves on the garment and use silk pins to pin the elements in place. Use matching thread and hand sew the design to the garment.

(For best results, stitch elements in place from wrong side
of garment whenever possible.)

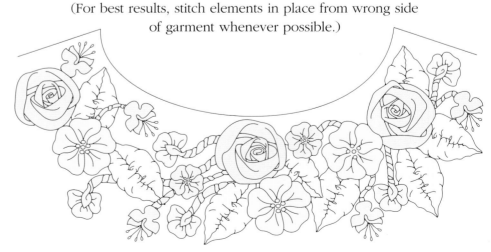

Design placement

An elegant floral-embellished headpiece can be made using simple wired ribbon and pearls.

Ribbon Floral Headpiece

Designed by Margaret Cox

INSTRUCTIONS

1. Cut mesh from one end of the teardrop headpiece to create a straight edge. Bend the wire from the frame along the cut edge of the mesh (trimming as necessary); re-glue the mesh to the wire edge.

2. Cut two pieces of satin about 1" larger on all sides than the frame. Fuse interfacing to the wrong sides of the satin shapes. Glue one satin shape to underside of the frame; trim the satin even with the edges. Wrapping the satin around the edges and pulling it taut, glue the remaining shape to the top of the frame, trimming the edges as needed.

3. Machine gather one long edge of the illusion to about a 6" to 7" width. Positioning the illusion evenly, hand sew the gathered edge of the illusion along the pointed end of the frame (back).

4. Glue gimp over the raw edges of the satin and gathered illusion on the underside of the headpiece.

cut away mesh here →

Cut mesh, bend wire, and re-glue.

5. Sew a length of elastic looping trim at the front underside edge of the headpiece. Insert the comb into the looping and sew in place.

6. For ribbon flowers, follow Making Ribbon Flowers: Loop Petal Flower (page 118) to make enough flowers to cover about ⅓ of the frame at the back point. Sew flowers to the headpiece.

7. Trim veiling to desired length.

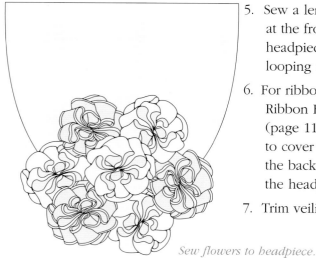

Sew flowers to headpiece.

SUPPLIES

1 yard 56" bridal illusion

Teardrop buckram headpiece frame

Ivory satin to cover both sides of frame

Lightweight fusible interfacing

Buttonhole twist thread to match fabric, trims, and ribbons

Clear hair comb

1¼ yards 1½" sheer wired ribbon

2½ yards 1" satin wired ribbon

1 yard narrow ivory decorative gimp

½ yard elastic looping trim

Pearl stamens

Craft glue

SUPPLIES

Sage green dress with scoop
  neckline
1 yard each of 1½" and 1"
  lavender ombré wired ribbon
1 yard 1" light lavender satin
  wired ribbon
½ yard 1½" light lavender
  sheer ribbon
1 yard 1" green velvet wired
  ribbon
1½ yards 1" green ombré
  wired ribbon
Pearl stamens

Ribbon Flower Key

Fuchsia
three from 1½" light
lavender sheer
ribbon, with center
buds from 1" light
lavender satin
ribbon

Half Primrose
one from 1"
lavender ombré
ribbon

Half Primrose with
Stem and Calyx
two from 1"
lavender ombré,
five from 1" light
lavendar ribbon,
stem and calyx from
green ombré ribbon

Primrose
two from 1"
lavender ombré
ribbon

Large Ruffled-
Petal Flower
one from 1½"
lavender ombré
ribbon

Folded Leaf
five from green
ombré ribbon

Gathered Leaf
five from green
velvet ribbon

*Ribbon work
embellishment
transforms simple
dresses into
something very
special to wear on
a very special day.*

Lavender and Sage Bridesmaid Dress
Designed by June Wildash Decker

INSTRUCTIONS

Referring to the illustration below and the Ribbon Flower Key, follow Making Ribbon Flowers and Leaves (pages 118–122) to make flowers, leaves, and stems from specified ribbons. Using the illustration as a guide, arrange flowers and leaves on the garment and use silk pins to pin elements in place. Use matching thread and hand sew the design to garment. (For best results, stitch elements in place from wrong side of garment whenever possible.)

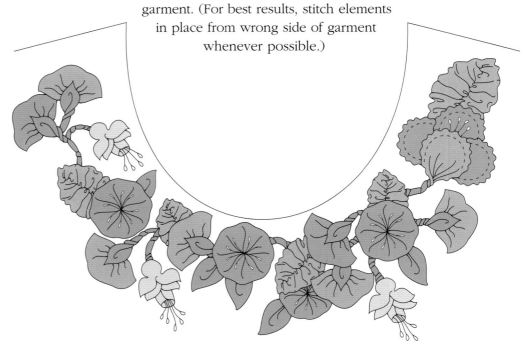

Design placement

Soft pastel variegated ribbon creates a lovely neckline on this bridesmaid's dress

Rosebud Bridesmaid Dress

Designed by
Kathy Pace

SUPPLIES

Ivory dress with scoop neckline
3 yards 1" pink-and-yellow
   variegated ribbon
3 yards each 3mm ivory, pale
   yellow, pale pink, and pale
   green silk ribbons
Perle cotton thread to match
   ribbons
Pearls

INSTRUCTIONS

Refer to illustrations and follow Stitch Key, Silk Ribbon Embroidery (page 115), and Making Ribbon Flowers: Crushed Rose (page 119) to make rosebuds, and stitch roses, stems, and leaves on neckline of dress and back of dress. If desired, use green perle cotton to stitch additional vines along design and leaves using lazy daisy and stem stitch.

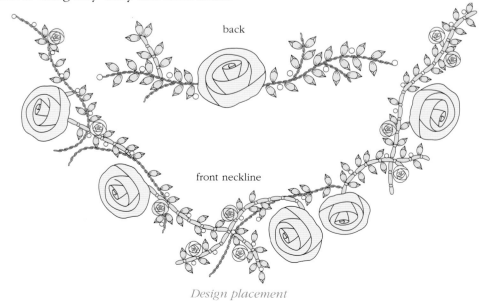

back

front neckline

Design placement

Stitch Key

 **Crushed Rosebud**
*pink variegated
ribbon*

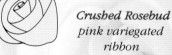 **Couching**
pale green

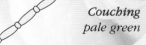 **Stem Stitch**
pale green

**Japanese Ribbon
Stitch**
pale green

 **Spider Web Rose**
*ivory, pale yellow,
and pink*

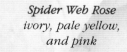 **Pearls**

Mother of the Bride Ensemble

Designed by Donna Martin

A silk blouse embellished with lace and silk ribbon embroidery and pieced vest accented with vintage laces, ribbon embroidery, and pearls make a beautiful ensemble for the mother of the bride.

Tiered Ruffles Skirt

SUPPLIES

3 yards 60" fabric or 4 yards
   45" fabric (we used rayon)
1 yard muslin
Thread to match fabric
1 yard 1¼" elastic
Fabric pencil
Heavy spray starch

INSTRUCTIONS

Note: Read all instructions before beginning. Pre-launder fabric before cutting skirt pieces. Sew ½" seams with fabric right sides together.

1. **For 60" fabric:** Match the selvage edges and cut a fabric length for the skirt body accordingly: 35" for petite, 37" for average, and 39" for tall.

2. For ruffles, cut eight 5½"-wide strips the width of the fabric (60"). Cut three of the strips in half to make six 30" long strips. Sew a 60" strip to a 30" strip to make an approximately 90" long strip; repeat to make four more strips.

3. **For 45" fabric:** Refer to Step 1 for skirt body length and cut two 30½" wide fabric lengths. Place the lengths together and sew along one long edge; press the seam open (piece should measure 60" wide). For ruffles, cut ten 5½"-wide fabric strips the width of fabric (45"). Sew ends of two strips together to make an approximately 90" long strip; repeat to make four more strips.

4. To construct the skirt, lay the skirt body on a flat surface and mark with a fabric pencil at 4½" intervals.

waist edge

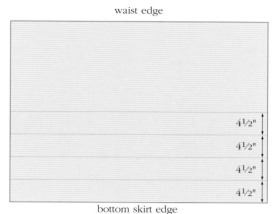

4½"
4½"
4½"
4½"

bottom skirt edge

Mark skirt body at 4½" intervals.

5. To hem each strip, press one long edge of the strip ¼" to wrong side; press again ¼" and sew close to the first pressed edge.

6. Use a long machine basting stitch and sew a line of stitching ¼" from the raw edge of each strip. Gather each strip to measure 60".

7. With the hemmed edge toward the waist edge, match the gathered edge of one ruffle to the bottom edge of the skirt body, right sides together; pin the ruffle to the skirt body. For the remaining ruffles, meet the gathered edge of one ruffle to each marked line; pin in place. Beginning and ending ½" from each end, sew the ruffles to the skirt body.

8. Keeping the ruffle ends free from stitching, match the long edges of the skirt body and sew. Sew the ends of the ruffles together where they meet at the skirt body seam and sew the remaining part of the ruffle to the skirt.

9. Zigzag or overlock the raw edges of the bottom of the skirt body and bottom ruffle. To conceal the raw edges of the remaining ruffles, fold the ruffles up against the skirt body. Sew a ½"-wide tuck on the wrong side of skirt, enclosing the raw edge of each remaining ruffle. Press the tuck toward the waist edge. Topstitch on the right side of the skirt just above the ruffles.

10. (Note: If the skirt is too long, cut the waistline edge to shorten the skirt, allowing for the waistband casing.) For the waistband, press the waist edge ¼" to the wrong side; press again 1¾". Leaving a 2"-wide opening for inserting elastic, sew along the first pressed edge to form the waistband casing. Measure your waist; add 1". Cut elastic this measurement. Insert elastic through the casing; overlap ½" and sew the ends of the elastic together. Sew the opening closed; adjust the waistband gathers.

To Wrinkle the Skirt

Wrinkling the skirt may be done by one person, but two can make the task easier and faster.

Cut 2" to 3" wide muslin strips and sew the ends together to make a 6' to 10' long strip.

Dampen the skirt with heavy spray starch (use at least ⅓ of a large can). Gather the waist of skirt in one hand and tie with the muslin strip. Wrap the skirt tightly with the muslin strip, squeezing and making sure the pleats formed by the gathers are tight as you wrap (muslin wrap should be flat and cover most of skirt). Tie off the muslin strip at the bottom of skirt.

Bake the wrapped skirt in the oven at 125° to 150° overnight. Unwrap the skirt and shake out.

To maintain the crinkled look of the skirt when laundered, twist the laundered skirt and place it in a leg of a pantyhose and allow to dry: keep it in the hose until ready to wear.

Vintage Vest

INSTRUCTIONS

1. Make any necessary fitting adjustments to the vest pattern. Reversing the vest front pattern for left and right fronts, trace the vest patterns onto tissue paper to make new left front, right front, and back templates. Cut out each template.

2. Keeping in mind that diagonal lines are more flattering, use a ruler to draw sections on the templates for piecing. Label the sections on each template "L" for left front, "R" for right front, or "B" for back. Number each section in the order to be sewn.

Vintage Vest back. (See additional photos page 38)

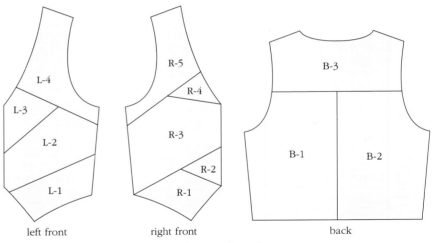

Draw sections on the templates for piecing.

3. Cut the template sections apart along the drawn lines for both fronts and the back.

4. *Note: Add ⅝" seam allowance to each edge where the template was cut apart before cutting the sections from fabric.*

   For the lace overlay, place the lace over the satin and pin in place. Cut the desired section(s) from the overlayed satin. Cut the remaining sections from the desired fabrics.

Cut template sections apart.

SUPPLIES

Favorite lined vest pattern
Fabrics and lace for pieced vest and lining (We used silk brocade, pink satin with lace overlay, and other fabrics for vest and brocade for lining.)
Assorted flat trims, appliqués, and doily laces (We used lace motifs cut from an heirloom wedding dress and other vintage laces.)
Pearl trim for vest edges
1⅞" bridal lace trim for bottom edges of vest
Assorted pearls
Iridescent sequins
4mm pink, dark pink, and green silk ribbons
Pink perle cotton thread
Tissue paper

5. Before piecing the sections together, determine if the lace trims will be inserted into sewn seams or appliquéd on top of the finished seam. With right sides together and lace trim inserted into seam allowance (if desired), sew the sections together in the numbered order to make the fronts and back of the vest.

6. Referring to the illustrations as a guide, follow Silk Ribbon Embroidery (page 115) to stitch flowers and leaves on the desired lace pieces or motifs. Sew pearls onto the laces.

7. Sew embellished laces and other laces, and pearls to the vest.

8. Baste pearl trim along the seamlines of the outer edges of the vest.

9. Follow the vest pattern instructions to assemble the lining and sew to the pieced vest. A zipper foot may be helpful when sewing the outer edges of the vest to stitch as close to the pearl trim as possible.

10. Sew bridal lace trim around the bottom edge of the vest.

Silk ribbon embroidery on motifs

Embroidery on motifs

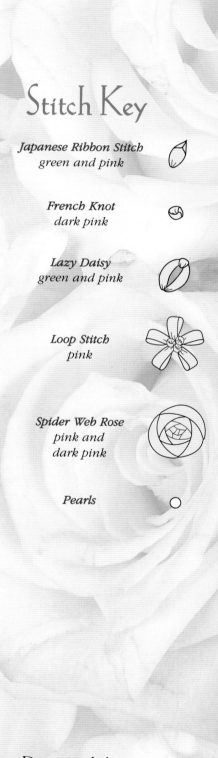

Stitch Key

Japanese Ribbon Stitch
green and pink

French Knot
dark pink

Lazy Daisy
green and pink

Loop Stitch
pink

Spider Web Rose
pink and dark pink

Pearls

Heart Shoulder Bag
Designed by Ninette Gehle

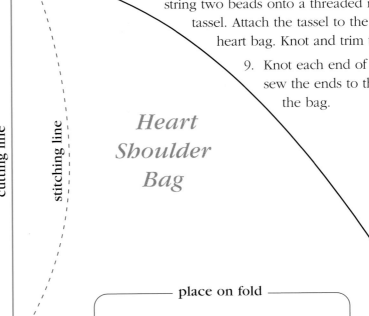

A pretty heart-shaped or drawstring bag is a loving handmade accessory for the bride or bridesmaids to carry.

INSTRUCTIONS

1. Trace the heart pattern onto tracing paper; cut out.

2. Cut two hearts from taffeta and one heart from batting.

3. For the pocket, use the part of the heart template below the red line and cut two shapes from taffeta.

4. Transfer the curved stitching line on the pattern to the wrong side of one pocket piece. Sew the pocket pieces right sides together along the drawn stitching line. Clip the curves and turn the pocket to the right side; press.

5. Sew laces, buttons, and beads to one side of the pocket and the top of one taffeta heart.

6. Layer embellished heart and pocket pieces right sides up, remaining taffeta heart wrong side up, and batting heart. Leaving an opening for turning, sew the layers together using a ¼" seam allowance. Trim the seam, turn to the right side, and press. Hand sew the opening closed.

7. Hand sew fold-over trim around the outer edge of the bag.

8. For the tassel, take a stitch at the top of the tassel; string two beads onto a threaded needle at the tassel. Attach the tassel to the bottom of the heart bag. Knot and trim the thread.

9. Knot each end of the cord and sew the ends to the top back of the bag.

SUPPLIES

¼ yard cream moiré taffeta

Low-loft polyester batting

⅔ yard ⅞" fold-over decorative trim

1½ yards ¼"-diameter twisted rayon cord

Assorted lace appliqués and motifs

Assorted pearl buttons and beads

3" tassel

Tracing paper

Transfer paper

cutting line

stitching line

Heart Shoulder Bag

place on fold

Taffeta Drawstring Bag
Designed by Ninette Gehle

(Photo page 42)

INSTRUCTIONS

1. Cut 1"-wide lace into four equal lengths. Overlapping edges slightly, arrange 1"- and 2"-wide lace pieces on the lower half of the taffeta piece (front of bag); sew the top edges of each lace length to the bag. Sew the trim along the edge of the top lace piece.

2. Matching right sides and using a ¼" seam allowance, sew the short edges of the lining to the short edges of the taffeta piece; press the seams open.

3. Meet seams of sewn tube with lining to one side and taffeta to the opposite side. Refer to the illustration to sew the side seams of the lining and bag, leaving a small opening in the lining for turning the bag and one ⅜" opening on each side of the bag for the drawstring casing openings.

4. Turn the bag to the right side. Sew the opening in the lining closed. Insert the lining into the bag (about 1¾" of taffeta should turn to the inside at the top of the bag).

5. For the drawstring casing, start at one side of the bag at the top of the casing opening and sew a line of stitching around the bag. Sew a second line of stitching ⅜" below the first line of stitching.

6. For the drawstring, cut two 14" lengths of cord. Attach a small safety pin to one end of one cord length and insert the cord into the casing; push the cord through the casing, exiting at the same entry point. Remove the pin and knot the ends of the cord together. Repeat to thread the second cord length through casing, entering and exiting the casing at the opposite side of the bag. Sew pearls and beads to each knot.

7. For the handles, cut the remaining cord in half. Hold the cords together and knot one end. Twist the cord to desired effect; knot the remaining ends together. Sew the knots inside the bag at each side.

8. Sew additional jewels and ribbon roses to the front of the bag.

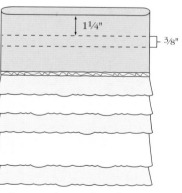

Sew side seams.

Sew two lines of stitching.

SUPPLIES

6½" x 20" blue moiré taffeta
6½" x 14" lining fabric
¾ yard 1" vintage lace
6½" of 2" vintage lace
6½" of ⅛" decorative trim
4½ yards ⅛"-diameter ivory twisted cord
Assorted pearls, crystal beads, and pieces from antique jewelry
3 small pink ribbon roses

Bridesmaid Brunch

A peach-flavored beverage is a wonderful treat.

A Reminiscent Affair

The bridesmaid brunch is a special gathering to celebrate the bride and her attendants. Lighthearted decorations and luscious refreshments make the bridal gathering memorable. In sentimental fashion, favorite refreshments and handmade accents are perfect choices for a beautiful brunch or bridal shower. Beginning with the invitation, select a treasured family photograph as a symbol of ageless love to grace the front of the card. Here, the wedding picture of the bride's grandparents was photocopied onto the front of the invitation. For quaint decorations, reminders of child's play are never far away, with whimsical dolls and bears in complete wedding gala. These miniature brides and grooms set the stage at the brunch entrance and make wonderful party table accents. Handmade gifts complete the brunch celebration. Simple sachets sewn from elegant vintage fabrics and trims are lovely friendship favors for the bridesmaids.

An heirloom photograph adds a romantic touch to a wedding event.

-Amy's Great Grandparents-
FREITAG
1911

What: Bridal Gathering honoring Amy Martin
When: September 16, 1995
Where: 7219 Franklin
Time: 9:30am to 11:30am
Kay Wright
Gwen Znerold
Regrets only: 278-5745 • 276-8204

Whimsical soft-sculptured dolls are wonderful decorations for any wedding occasion.

Dignified Wedding Couple
Designed by Ruth Cox

INSTRUCTIONS
Note: Soft sculpture is achieved by stuffing a shape and using a needle to position stuffing into a feature and securing the feature with small stitches. You may want to practice making facial features on a test face before making the doll. Sew ¼" seams with fabric right sides together unless otherwise stated.

SUPPLIES

(for two 26" dolls)

One pair nylon pantyhose
½ yard muslin
Polyester fiber fill
10-12 small silk flowers
White, blue, brown, and black
  acrylic paint
Small round paintbrush
Red and black
  permanent markers
Eight 18" lengths of white
  18-gauge wire for legs and
  arms
Cosmetic blush
2 craft sticks
Tracing paper
Dressmakers' tracing paper
Soft sculpture needle

FOR GROOM

½ yard fabric for suit
5" square fabric for bow tie
3 small buttons to match muslin
3 small buttons to match suit
  fabric
Approximately 4"–4½" pur-
  chased black felt doll hat
  to fit groom
One package brown wool
  roving for hair
One 18" length of black
  18-gauge wire for glasses

FOR BRIDE

½ yard each vintage lace and
  sheer fabric for bride's dress
  and veil
1 yard 1½" ivory satin ribbon
1¼ yards ¼" ivory ribbon
½ yard ivory narrow twisted
  rayon cord
One package yellow wool
  roving for hair
8" of string pearls

GROOM

1. For the head, cut a 4½" section of pantyhose (do not use the foot area). Hand sew a curved line to form chin.

Sew curved line for chin.

2. Trim excess pantyhose around chin. Turn shape to the right side, stuff with fiber fill to an approximate 3½" circumference, and hand sew the top of the head closed.

Stitch ear

3. For each ear, pull up stuffing in an ear shape at the side of the head and hand sew two rows of small stitches through the ear.

4. For the nose, find the center of the face and pull up a section of stuffing. Referring to the illustration, stitch evenly back and forth under the raised section. For each nostril, take a stitch from the side of the nose to the bottom of the nose.

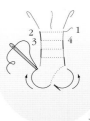

Stitch nose

5. For the mouth, stitch a curved line; hand sew small stitches below the line to form the lower lip. Sew back and forth from the upper lip area to the lower lip two to three times.

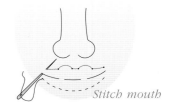

Stitch mouth

6. For each eyelid, pull up a small section of stuffing and make small stitches through the section to form a half-moon shape. For the eyes, paint small white circles under the eyelids. Paint brown irises and black pupils. Paint a white dot in each pupil for highlight.

Stitch eyelids

7. Use a black marker to color the eyebrows and draw eyeliner. Use blush to color the cheeks and mouth.

8. Refer to the illustration for hair placement. Cut an approximate 5" square of hair material and hand sew the hair to the head around the face, behind ears, and along back neck edge (creating a part at one side and two sideburns).

Hair placement

9. Trace the torso, arm, leg (extending pattern as stated), and suit patterns onto tracing paper; then cut out.

10. Use the templates to cut the indicated number of shapes for the torso, arms, legs, and shirt front, back, and collar from muslin. Cut suit jacket and pant pieces from fabric.

11. For the torso, sew side, shoulder, and lower curved edges together; turn to the right side. Stuff the torso firmly. Sew across each hip where the leg extension meets the torso (dashed line). Stuff to the end of the leg extensions; sew the openings closed.

12. For each arm and leg, sew two of each shape together, leaving the top open; turn right side out. Stuff each arm firmly. Insert a wire length from the top of the arm to the fingertips. Refer to the pattern to stitch three lines for fingers on the hand. Attach the arms to the sides of the torso. For the legs, stuff each shape to the knee (dashed line); stitch across each leg at the knee. Stuff the remaining part of leg. Attach the legs to the leg extensions on the torso.

13. Place one craft stick into the torso extending about 1½" of the stick from the neck. Cut a slit in the doll head just behind the chin and insert the head onto the stick. Hand sew the head to the torso.

14. Paint the shoes black. Paint white laces on shoes.

15. Sew the jacket front and back shapes together at the shoulders. Press the center front edges of the jacket ¼" to the wrong side. Fold the jacket collar in half lengthwise and sew each end; turn to the right side. Inserting the neck edge of the jacket into the collar opening, sew the collar to the jacket. Turn the collar down over the jacket and tack in place. Sew the sleeves to the jacket armholes. Sew sleeve and side seams. Hem the lower edges of the jacket and sleeves.

16. Sew the pant shapes together at the sides and inner edges; turn right side out. Hem each pant leg.

17. Sew the shirt front and back together at the shoulders. Press the center front edges of the shirt ¼" to the wrong sides. Place the shirt on the doll, overlapping the front edges. Fold the collar in half lengthwise and sew each end; turn right side out. Inserting the neck edge of the shirt into the collar opening, hand sew the collar to the shirt. Make a tuck in the back of the shirt to fit the shirt to the doll. Overlap the front and back at the sides and hand sew the shirt to the doll. Sew three buttons onto the shirt.

18. Cut a 2" x 4" piece of fabric for the tie and a 1" square for the tie center. Bring the long edges of the tie to the center. Bring the ends to the center and baste together. Press two edges of the tie center to the wrong side and wrap the center piece around the tie to form the bow; hand sew the ends together at the back of tie. Tack the bow tie to the front of the collar.

19. Place the suit on the groom, hand sewing it to the doll if necessary. Overlap the fronts of jacket and sew three buttons to close the jacket. Sew a small bunch of silk flowers to one collar. Shape a 6" length of black wire into glasses and place on the doll; tack the glasses in place on the face. Place the hat on the head.

BRIDE

1. Follow Steps 1 through 7 of the groom instructions, painting blue irises for eyes and using a red marker to color the lips.

2. For the hair, cut a 6" square of hair material and back comb to create volume. Refer to the illustration and hand sew the hair to the head around the face, and turn the hair ends under to form a pouf at the ears; sew the pouf to the head.

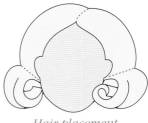

Hair placement.

3. Use only the torso, leg, and arm patterns and follow Steps 9 through 13 of the groom instructions, cutting the torso from the pantyhose. Use the elastic band from the pantyhose to tie around doll's waist for additional shaping.

4. Paint shoes white.

5. For the underdress, cut a 13" x 16½" piece of sheer fabric. Fold the fabric piece in half lengthwise. Cut a neckline curve at one short edge of the fabric; cut 2" armhole openings at each side near the top. Sew the long raw edge from the bottom of the armhole to the bottom of the dress. Place the underdress on the doll; hand sew together at the shoulders.

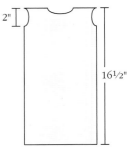

Cut neckline and armholes.

6. For the lace dress, cut an 18" square and two 4½" x 5½" pieces of lace. Repeat Step 5 to cut and sew the lace dress (we used the scallop edges of lace for the lower edges of dress and sleeves). Fold each sleeve piece in half and sew the long raw edges together. Sew the sleeves into the lace dress armholes.

7. For the overskirt, cut an 11" x 18" piece of the same lace and sew the short edges together. Place the overskirt over the lace dress with the top raw edges at the waist. Use a running stitch to gather the overskirt and lace dress together at the waist.

8. Tie 1½"-wide ribbon around the waist and add lace trims around the neckline and along the ribbon. Tie pearls around the neck for a necklace. Knot the remaining ¼"-wide ribbon and twisted rayon cord around a small bouquet of flowers. Glue flowers to each end of the ribbon and cord. Attach the bouquet to one hand.

9. For the veil, cut an 18" square of lace and round one edge (bottom). Use a running stitch to gather the lace into a circle from the middle of the lace to the top of the lace to fit the crown of doll's head. Attach the veil to the head. Embellish with lace trim and small flowers.

Patterns for the Dignified Wedding Couple begin on page 50.

A fine dessert of mouth-watering chocolate cannot be turned down.

A peach-flavored beverage is a wonderful treat.

Creamy Chocolate Celeste

8-ounce package semi-sweet chocolate
1-ounce square unsweetened chocolate
2 Tablespoons butter or margarine
2 Tablespoons strong coffee
Few grains salt
2 eggs, separated
1 Tablespoon brandy
2 cups whipping cream
Your choice of garnish: shaved chocolate, finely chopped
  walnuts, or candied edible flowers

Melt chocolates with the butter in a double boiler pan over boiling water; stir to blend until smooth. Remove from heat. Stir in coffee, salt, egg yolks, and brandy. Beat egg whites until stiff; fold gently into chocolate mixture slowly, but thoroughly. Whip cream until it mounds softly but is not stiff. Fold cream into chocolate mixture until a marbled effect is obtained. Spoon into dessert dishes, mounding high. Chill for several hours. If desired, garnish with small swirls of additional whipped cream, shaved chocolate, sprinkles of finely chopped walnuts, or candied edible flowers.

Makes 8 half-cup servings

Peachy Pleasure

10-ounce package of frozen peaches;
  or 4 fresh peaches peeled, pitted, and sliced
½ cup super fine sugar
½ cup peach liqueur or brandy
2 liters champagne
1 liter club soda
Peaches or mint leaves
  for garnish

Thaw the frozen peaches to room temperature. Combine peaches, sugar, and liqueur in an electric blender; process until smooth. Pour into a large pitcher. Slowly pour remaining ingredients over peach mixture and stir gently. Garnish with mint leaves or sliced fresh peaches. Serve immediately.

Makes approximately 12–14 one-cup servings

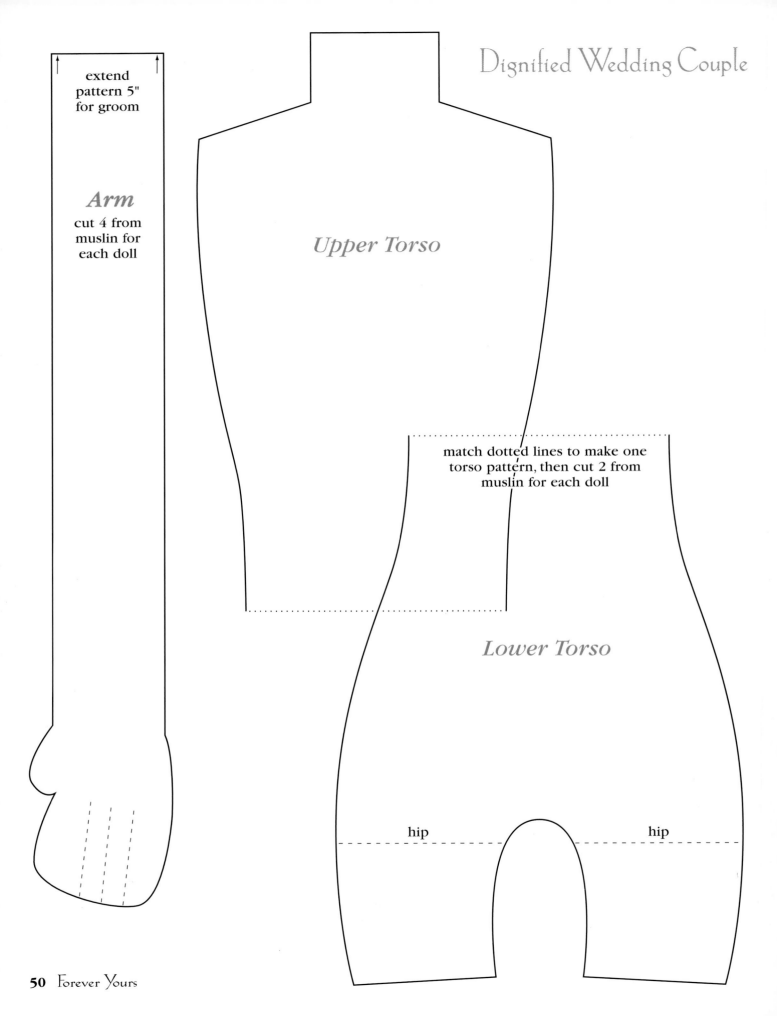

extend
pattern 5"
for groom

Arm

cut 4 from
muslin for
each doll

Dignified Wedding Couple

Upper Torso

match dotted lines to make one
torso pattern, then cut 2 from
muslin for each doll

Lower Torso

hip

hip

Dignified Wedding Couple (continued)

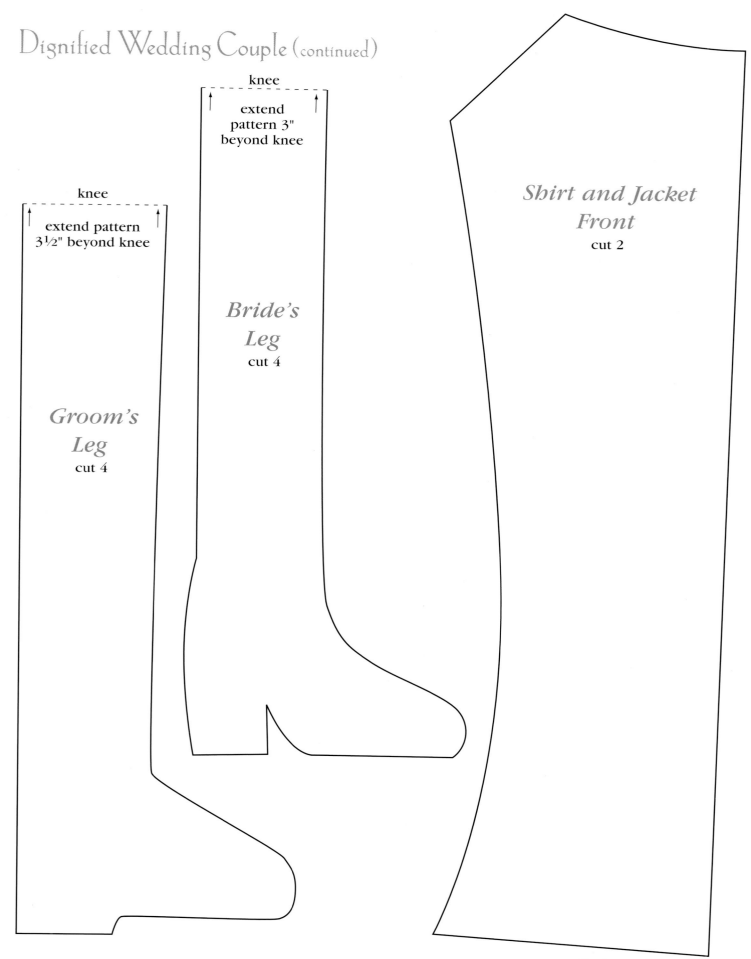

knee

extend
pattern 3"
beyond knee

**Bride's
Leg**
cut 4

knee

extend pattern
3½" beyond knee

**Groom's
Leg**
cut 4

*Shirt and Jacket
Front*
cut 2

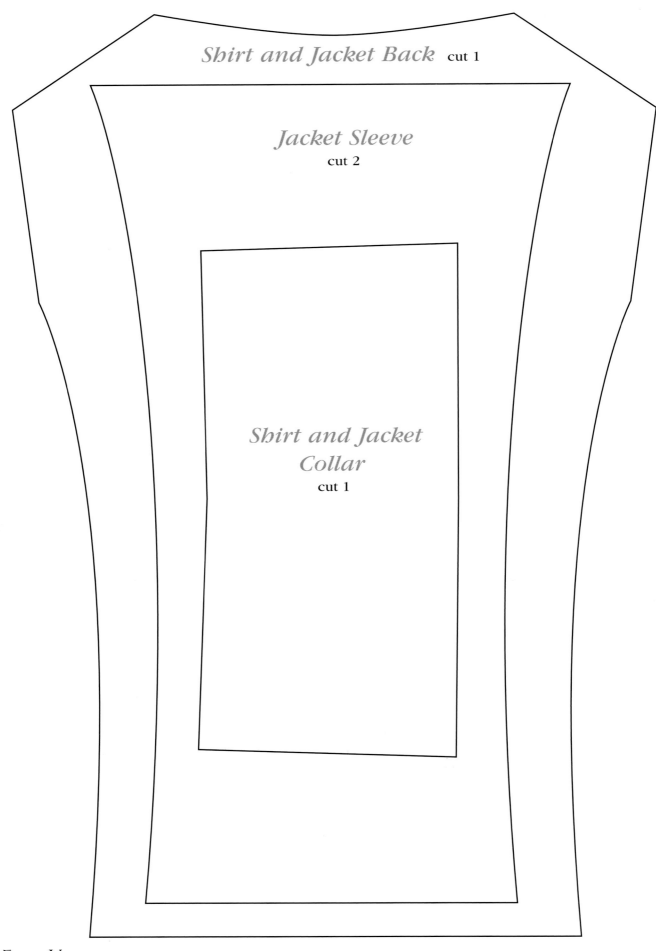

Shirt and Jacket Back cut 1

Jacket Sleeve
cut 2

*Shirt and Jacket
Collar*
cut 1

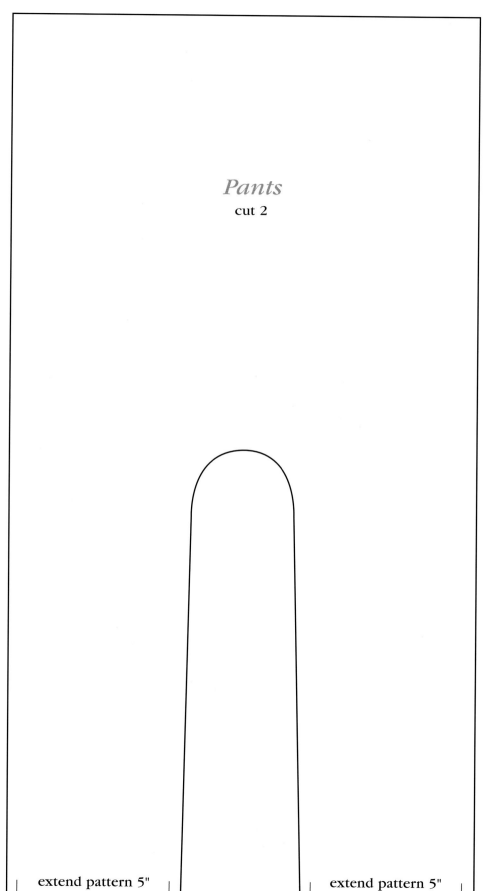

Pants
cut 2

extend pattern 5"   extend pattern 5"

A delightful welcome!

Designed by Ruth Cox

This crafted bride greets brunch guests at the door in a sheath gown recreated from an old lace curtain. A metal doll stand gives her perfect posture and makes her a treasure to be displayed long after the wedding day. To make this doll, refer to the Dignified Wedding Couple instructions (beginning on page 45), enlarging the body patterns 200% to make a 44" doll. Use the additional supplies and instructions here to construct the doll and make her lacy bridal dress and veil.

INSTRUCTIONS

1. For the head, use a 7" section of stocking and follow Steps 1 through 8 of Dignified Wedding Couple groom instructions (beginning on page 45). Stuff the head with fiber fill to an approximate 5" circumference.

2. For the body, enlarge the torso, bride's leg, and arm patterns by 200% (copiers may differ, so make sure enlarged pattern will make a 44" doll); cut out. Cut the indicated number of torso and arm shapes from muslin. Cut the legs from white stockings. Follow Steps 9 through 13 of the groom instructions (page 47) to construct the doll body.

ADDITIONAL SUPPLIES

(see supply list, page 46, for basic materials to make the doll)

1½ yards muslin (replaces muslin requirement from page 46 list)

White cotton or wool stockings for legs

Two 12" x 36" fabric pieces for underdress

Two 12" x 36" and two 6" x 16" pieces of lace for dress

8" of 2½" lace trim for collar

¾ yard fine netting for veil

½ yard ¼" satin ribbon

6-7 small silk flowers

14" of teardrop-shape string pearls for necklace

10" of small, round string pearls for veil

3. For the lace dress, start about 4" from one short edge and sew the long edges of the large lace pieces together. Cut a 4"-wide neckline curve at the center top. Cut a slight angle from each side of the neckline to the edge of lace (shoulders). Repeat to make the underdress. Place the underdress inside the lace dress; baste together at the shoulders. Place the dress on the doll. Turning the edges under, sew the dress together at the shoulders.

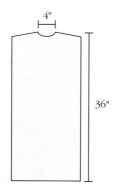

Cut neckline and shoulder angle.

4. For the sleeves, fold each remaining lace piece in half and sew the long edges together; turn right side out. Hand sew the sleeve to the dress at the armhole. Overlapping the edges, sew the 2½"-wide lace piece around the neckline for the collar.

5. Tie 14" of teardrop string pearls around the neck for a necklace. Sew a bow made from ¼" satin ribbon to the top of each shoe.

6. For the veil, fold netting in half from side to side; fold in half again from top to bottom. Cut, rounding the raw edges of the netting; unfold. Use a running stitch to gather around the edges of half of the netting piece. Attach the veil to the head along the gathered edges. Insert small flowers on each side of the veil. Sew 10" of small round string pearls to the top of the veil. Tuck the back edges of the veil up and under the flowers; sew to secure.

To be loved, be lovable.

Ovid
The Art of Love. II, Line 107

A cherished antique doll dressed as a bride is a charming table accent.

Victorian Bride Doll Dress and Veil *Designed by Donna Martin*

SUPPLIES
(for an approximately 22" doll)

FOR DRESS
- ½ yard ivory satin
- ½ yard ivory fabric for underlining
- 1½ yards 4½" vintage lace for collar and lower edge of gown and other assorted laces (We used vintage lace from an heirloom wedding dress, appliqués, tatted trims, and doilies.)
- Assorted round and iris pearls
- Tracing paper

FOR VEIL
- 1 yard ivory tulle
- 2½ yards ½" ivory ribbon
- Craft barrette
- Hot glue gun and glue sticks

INSTRUCTIONS
Note: Sew ¼" seams with fabric right sides together unless otherwise stated.

DRESS

1. Trace dress patterns onto tracing paper; cut out. Use the dress templates to cut the indicated number of shapes from each satin and underlining fabric. Cut the following additional pieces from each satin and underlining fabric: one 15" x 17½" piece for the skirt back, one 15" x 14½" piece for the skirt front, and two 4½" squares for the lower sleeves.

2. Sew one lower sleeve square to one underlining square along one matched edge; turn right side out and press. Repeat for the remaining lower sleeve squares.

3. (*Note: For the remainder of construction place each underlining fabric shape on the wrong side of like satin shape and work as if you are using one fabric shape, unless otherwise stated.*) Sew darts at lower edges of front and back bodice shapes. Sew the bodice back to the bodice front at the shoulders. Press each center back edge ¼" to the wrong side.

4. Use a running stitch to gather the lower edge of each sleeve shape. Match each gathered sleeve edge to the raw edges of one lower sleeve; sew the sleeve pieces together. Use a running stitch to gather the curved edge at the top of the sleeve. Pin the sleeves to the armhole edges and sew the sleeves to the bodice.

5. For the skirt back, place the satin skirt back and underlining pieces right sides together. Refer to the illustration and draw a 3" line at the center of one long edge (top) of the layered skirt pieces. Starting ¼" from the line, use a short stitch length and sew along the line forming a V. Cut along the drawn line to just within the bottom of the V; turn the skirt back right side out and press.

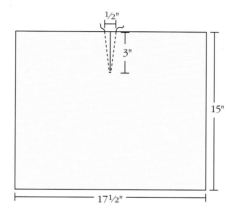

Sew the line forming a V.

6. Use a running stitch to gather the top edges of the skirt back and the top edge of the skirt front. Adjusting the gathers, pin the skirt back to the lower edges of the bodice back and the skirt front to the lower edge of the bodice front; sew the skirt to the bodice.

7. Matching seams and raw edges, sew each side seam of the dress; turn right side out.

8. For the ruffle at the neck edge, cut a 24" length of 4½" lace. Press and stitch the ends ¼" to the wrong side. Use a running stitch to gather the straight edge of the lace to fit the bodice neck edge; baste lace, right side up, to the neck edge.

9. For neck binding, cut a 1" wide satin strip ½" longer than the neck edge; press the ends and one long edge of the strip ¼" to the wrong side. Matching the pressed ends of the strip to the pressed center back edges and raw edge to neck raw edge, sew the strip along the neck edge over the gathered lace. Press the strip over the raw edge to the wrong side and stitch the pressed edge of the strip to the bodice.

10. Sew the remaining wide lace around the lower edge of the skirt. Sew additional lace trims around the sleeve edges and bodice. Attach a line of iris pearls along the center of the bodice. Embellish additional laces with pearls and hand sew to the skirt.

11. After the dress is on the doll, hand sew the back opening closed.

VEIL

1. For the veil, cut a 20" wide tulle piece 10" longer than height of doll. For ruffles, cut two 5" x 20" strips of tulle.

2. Sew ribbon along the long edges of the 5" x 20" tulle strips and along one short edge (top) of veil piece.

3. Refer to the illustration below to stack tulle strips at top of veil piece. Use a running stitch to gather layers together along center of ruffle strips.

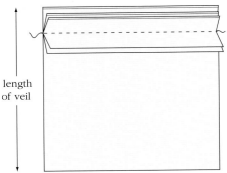

Stack tulle strips and gather.   *Gather to fit barrette width.*

4. Gather the veil to fit the width of the barrette; secure the gathers. Hot glue the veil to the top of the barrette.

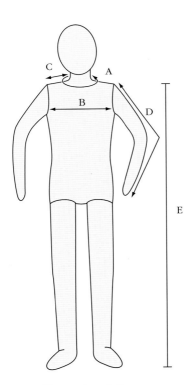

Measuring doll

Although the patterns for this doll's gown are for a 22" doll, you can adapt the patterns to fit any doll. Follow this diagram to measure your doll at the neck (A), torso front and back (B), shoulder line (C), arm length (D), and the height of doll from shoulder to foot (E).

Make alterations to the patterns provided using your doll's measurements.

Victorian Bride Doll

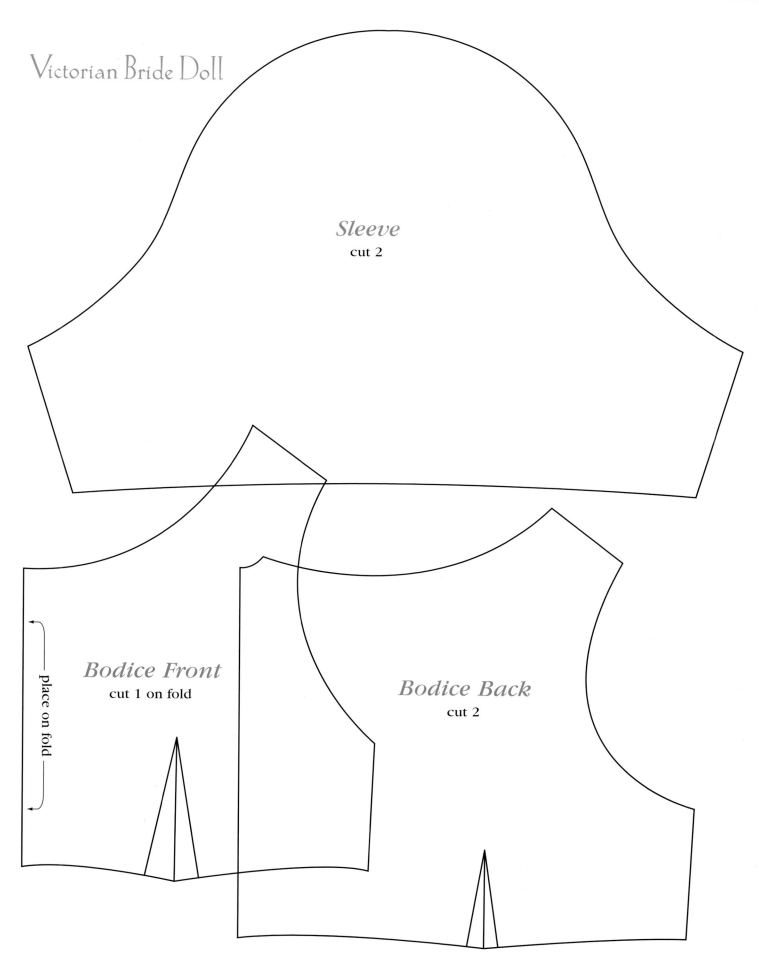

Sleeve
cut 2

Bodice Front
cut 1 on fold

place on fold

Bodice Back
cut 2

Dress up your favorite teddy bears for the occasion.

Bride and Groom Teddy Bears Attire
Designed by Donna Martin

SUPPLIES
(for approximately 19" bears)
Tracing paper

FOR BRIDE
1 yard lightweight ivory fabric
  and assorted vintage laces
  for dress
23" x 25" piece of vintage lace
  and 23" of 4" lace for veil
3 yards ½" ivory ribbon
Elastic cord
Miniature bouquet

FOR GROOM
½ yard purple velvet
1 yard 1" ivory satin
  crinkled ribbon
1 yard 4" lace for sleeve
  cuffs and jabot
Two ½" buttons
Antique doll boots and
  top hat to fit bear

INSTRUCTIONS

BRIDE
Note: Sew ¼" seams with fabric right sides together unless otherwise stated.

1. Trace the patterns onto tracing paper; cut out. Use the dress templates to cut the indicated number of shapes from the fabric. Cut an additional 16½" x 52" fabric piece for the skirt (piecing the width if necessary).

2. For the dress bodice, sew the front and back bodice shapes together at the shoulders.

3. For the sleeves, use a running stitch between the marks to gather the top of each sleeve to fit each armhole edge. Pin the sleeves to the bodice armhole matching the marks on the sleeves to the dots on the bodice. Sew the sleeves to the bodice leaving the sleeves unattached below the marks on

the sleeve. This allows ease for dressing the bear. Roll the bottom edges of the sleeves to the wrong side enclosing the raw edge and hand stitch in place. Cut two lengths of elastic cord to fit around the bear's wrists. Zigzag over one elastic cord about 2" from the hemmed edge of each sleeve; secure the elastic ends. Sew the underarm seams of the sleeves.

4. To attach the skirt, use a running stitch to gather the top edge of the skirt starting and ending ½" from each short edge. Match the raw edges, pin the skirt to the bodice and pull the gathering thread until the skirt fits around the bodice and under the open area of the sleeves. Sew the skirt to the bodice keeping the open area of the sleeves free.

5. Sew the lower 13½" of the skirt's center back seam together. Press the remaining center back seam ¼" to the wrong side and sew close to the pressed edges.

6. To hem the skirt, press the bottom edge of the skirt ¼" to the wrong side; press ¼" again and sew close to the first pressed edge.

7. Sew laces and ribbon to the bodice and skirt as desired. Place the dress on the bear. Tie a 10" length of ½" ivory ribbon into a bow around each wrist. Place the small bouquet in the bear's hand.

8. For the veil, fold one finished edge (top) of lace down about 4". Using the 23" length of 4" lace and referring to the illustration below, center the lace on the folded part of veil. Use a running stitch to gather the center of the laces until the veil fits between the ears of the bear; secure the gathers.

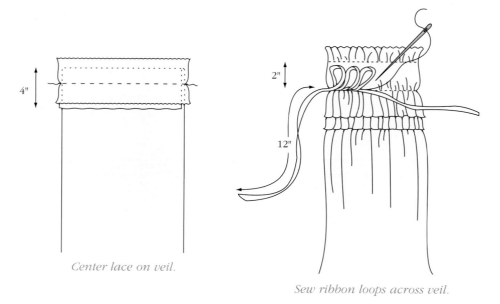

Center lace on veil.

Sew ribbon loops across veil.

9. Starting and ending with 12" streamers, sew 2" loops of ½" ivory ribbon across the gathered area of the veil. Hand sew the veil to the bear's head.

GROOM

Note: Sew ¼" seams with fabric right sides together unless otherwise stated.

1. Trace jacket patterns onto tracing paper; cut out. Use the jacket templates to cut out the indicated number of shapes from velvet.

2. Sew the jacket front and back together at the shoulders. Sew one front facing to each end of the back facing. Match the straight edges of each front jacket piece and front facing pieces right sides together. Sew the facing to the jacket along the neck, front, and bottom edges. Turn right side out.

3. For the jacket sleeves, use a running stitch to gather the top edges of the sleeves between the lines indicated on the pattern. Gather each sleeve to fit the armhole edges; pin in place and sew the sleeves to the jacket front and back. Cut two pieces from the lace to fit the lower edge of the sleeve for the cuffs. Fold each lace piece in half, meeting the long edges. With the finished edge of the lace on the right side of the sleeve, insert the lower edges of each sleeve into one folded lace piece; baste in place.

4. Sew the side seams of the jacket and sleeves, including the raw edges of the lace in the seam. Working from facing to facing, press the bottom raw edges of the jacket ¼" to the wrong side, mitering the corners at the jacket tails in the back; sew close to the pressed edge.

5. For the jabot, cut a 10" length from the lace and press the short edges ¼" to the wrong side; sew close to the pressed edges. Gather the straight edge (top) of the lace until the lace is about 4" wide; secure the gathers. Cut a 20" length from the crinkled ribbon. Center the gathered edge of the lace on the ribbon length, matching the gathered edge to one long edge of the ribbon. Sew the lace to the ribbon. Press the ribbon over the edge of the lace to the wrong side. Topstitch in place. Tie the remaining crinkled ribbon into a bow and tack to the jabot.

6. Place the jacket, hat, and boots on the bear. Overlap the center front edges of the jacket and turn the lapels back. Sew buttons to the center of the jacket. Tie the jabot around the bear's neck.

*The Love which moves the sun
and the other stars.*

—Dante Alighieri
*Divine Comedy. Purgatorio,
Canto XXXIII*

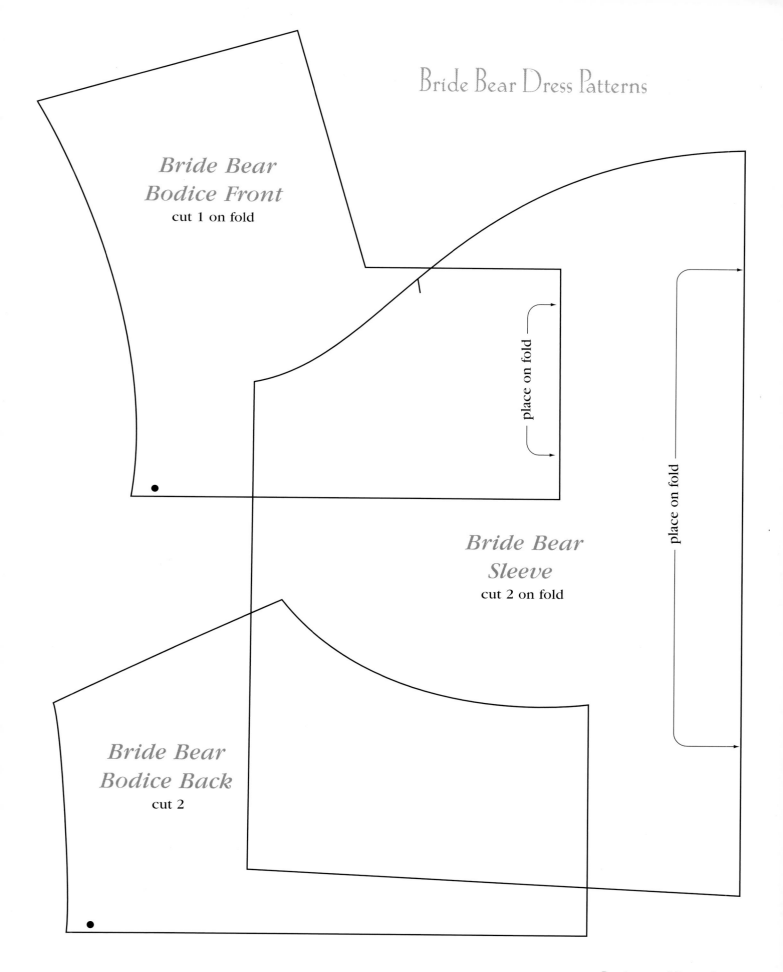

Bride Bear Dress Patterns

Bride Bear Bodice Front
cut 1 on fold

place on fold

place on fold

Bride Bear Sleeve
cut 2 on fold

Bride Bear Bodice Back
cut 2

Groom Bear Jacket Pattern

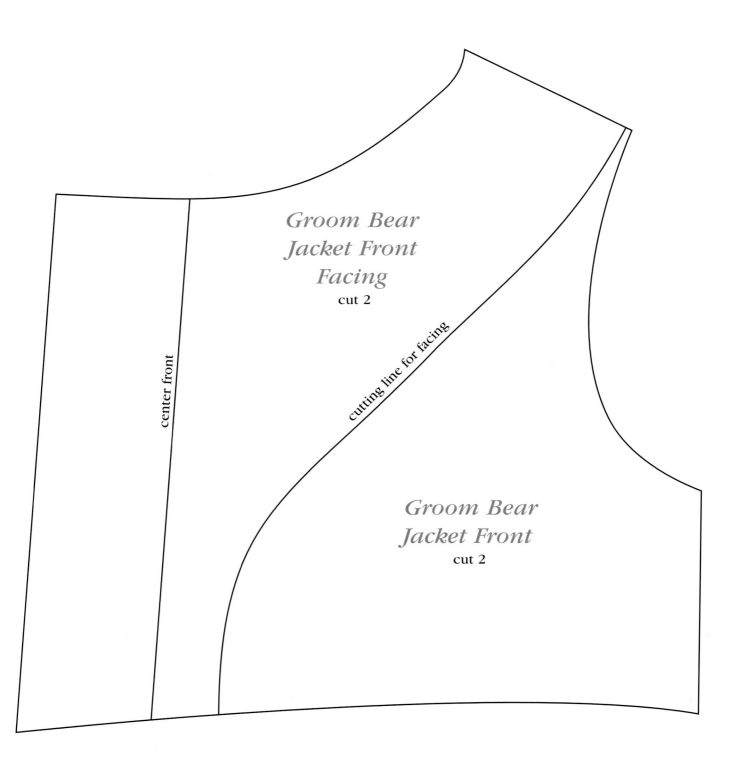

Groom Bear
Jacket Front
Facing
cut 2

center front

cutting line for facing

Groom Bear
Jacket Front
cut 2

Groom Bear Jacket Pattern (continued)

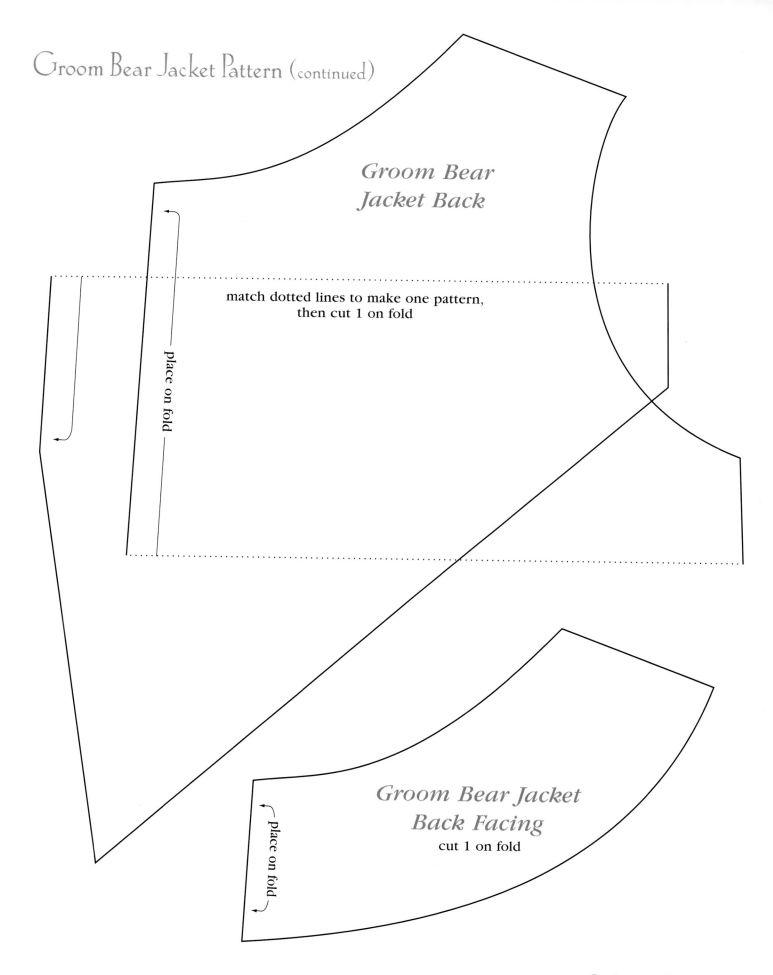

Groom Bear Jacket Back

match dotted lines to make one pattern, then cut 1 on fold

place on fold

Groom Bear Jacket Back Facing

cut 1 on fold

place on fold

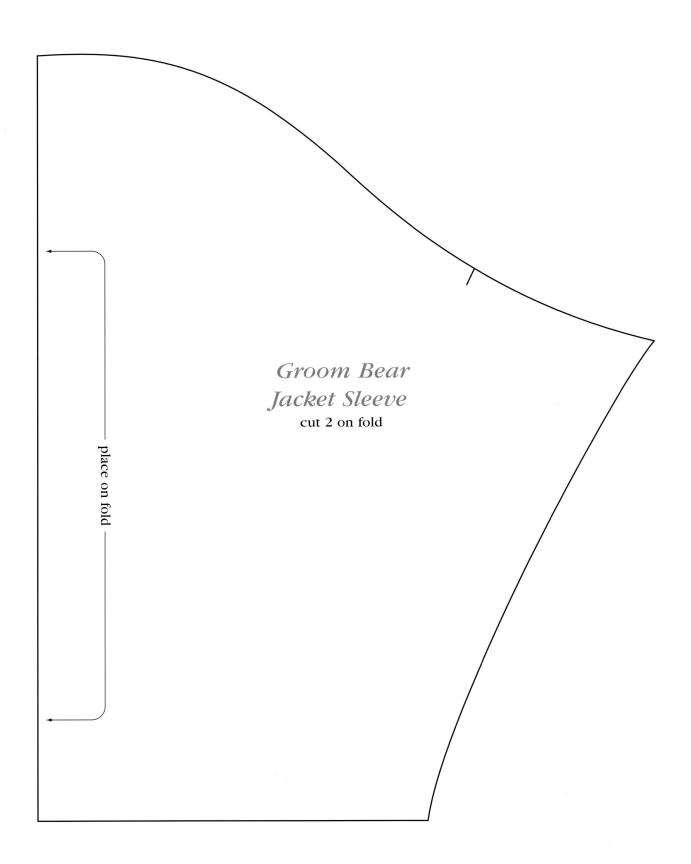

*Groom Bear
Jacket Sleeve*
cut 2 on fold

place on fold

A favor . . . sachets for the bridesmaids

Bridesmaid Favor Sachets

INSTRUCTIONS

1. To make each bag, meet the short ends of the fabric for the bag right sides together and sew using a ¼" seam; press the seam open. Center the seam on the fabric (center back of bag). Use a ¼" seam to sew the lower edge of the bag.

2. Repeat Step 1 for the lining fabric, except leave a 2" area in the middle of the first seam unsewn for turning bag right side out later. Turn the lining right side out.

3. Matching the right sides, center back seams, and top raw edges, insert the lining into the bag and sew around the top edges. Turn the bag right side out. Sew the opening in the lining closed. Insert the lining into the bag.

4. Hand sew trims and jewels to the bag as desired.

5. Place about ½ cup or more of potpourri into the bag.

6. For the tassel cord tie, cut a 10" twisted cord length. Cut two 3" pieces of fringe. Stitching as you go, wrap one fringe piece around one end of the cord; repeat for the remaining end of the cord. Knot the tassel cord around the top of the bag.

7. For bows, tie several 1-yard lengths ribbons and/or laces together into a bow around the top of the bag.

SUPPLIES

11" x 8½" each of fabric for bag and lining
Desired trims (We used vintage laces, ribbons, twisted cord, fringe, and jewels.)
Potpourri

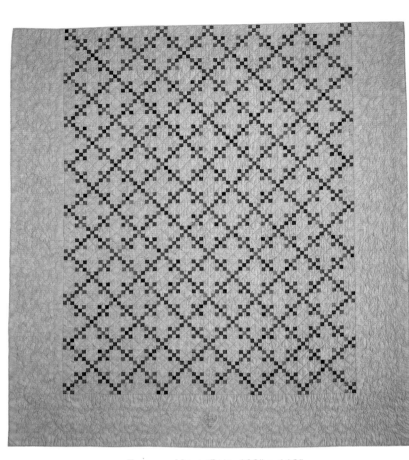

Forever, Marg Gair, 102" x 112",
three hundred three 3" finished Nine-Patch blocks.

Forever Quilt

Note from the designer, Marg Gair:

On our twenty-fifth wedding anniversary my husband presented me with a gold heart for my charm bracelet. On the front he had "Forever" engraved and on the back it had a passage from one of our favorite poems..."You are my north, my south, my east and west" by W.H. Auden. I was touched, and it inspired me to make a wedding quilt to commemorate our twenty-five years of marriage. This quilt, personalized with the bride and groom's names and marriage date would also be a wonderful gift for the wedding couple to celebrate their special day.

FABRIC TIPS: To achieve a traditional, aged appearance, use plaids, stripes, and small prints. This truly is a scrap quilt and looks best with a large number of different fabrics so there aren't numerous repeats in the nine-patches. The background fabric, although it almost looks like a muslin, has a wonderful golden patina which gives it an antique look. The nine-patches are made of browns and blues which are predominately medium and dark in value. However, bright medium to medium-light blues were used occasionally but consistently throughout to give this quilt some sparkle.

SUPPLIES

The following gives you the total yardage needed, assuming the fabric is at least 42" wide.

11 yards light fabric for nine-patch background, sashing, border, and binding

2¼ yards total of brown fabric

1¼ yards total of blue fabric

9 yards for backing

120" x 120" batting

Rotary cutter and mat

18" straight-edge ruler

Pigma micron™ permanent pen

INSTRUCTIONS

Nine-Patch Blocks

CUTTING

Note: For quick cutting, cut all of the quilt top fabrics (except borders) cross grain with a rotary cutter and cutting mat.

Light fabric for Nine-Patch blocks: Cut 48 1½"-wide strips across the width of fabric.

Browns for Nine-Patch blocks: Cut 40 1½"-wide strips across the width of fabric.

Blues for Nine-Patch blocks: Cut 20 1½"-wide strips across the width of fabric.

Light fabric for Alternate blocks: Cut 18 3½"-wide strips. Then cut the strips into 3½" squares. You will need a total of 192 3½" squares.

BLOCK ASSEMBLY

Note: Use ¼" seam allowance unless otherwise noted. Press seams toward the darker fabric.

1. Sew two dark strips and one light strip together; make 24 sets of light and medium/dark strips, using a wide variety of brown and blue fabric combinations. Cut into 1½" units.

1½"

Sew two dark strips and one light strip together.

2. Sew two light strips and one dark dark strip together; make 12 sets of light and medium/dark strips. Cut into 1½" units.

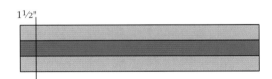

1½"

Sew two light strips and one dark dark strip together.

3. Sew the units together to make a total of 303 Nine-Patch blocks according to the diagram. The Double Nine-Patch Blocks will require 240 Nine-Patch blocks, while the remaining 63 will be used for the sashing posts.

9" Double Nine-Patch Blocks

BLOCK ASSEMBLY

4. Sew 240 of the Nine-Patch blocks into Double Nine-Patch blocks according to the diagram. This will give you 48 Double Nine-Patch blocks.

Sew the units together

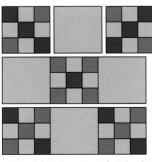

Double Nine-Patch Block

SASHING

5. Cut 10 9½"-wide strips across the width of the light fabric. Then cut the strips every 3½". You will need a total of 110 9½" x 3½" rectangles.

QUILT ASSEMBLY

6. Sew the Double Nine-Patch blocks into rows adding a sashing strip between each Double Nine-Patch block and at the beginning and end of each row. Sew the sashing and Nine-Patch posts into rows according to the diagram.

7. Sew the rows together.

BORDERS

Note: Cut borders along the lengthwise grain of fabric.

8. Measure the length of the quilt across the middle. Cut two borders the length of the quilt by 14" wide. Pin and sew the borders onto each side.

9. Measure the width of the quilt across the middle. Cut one border the width of the quilt by 14" wide. Pin and sew onto the bottom of the quilt.

10. Press the quilt top well.

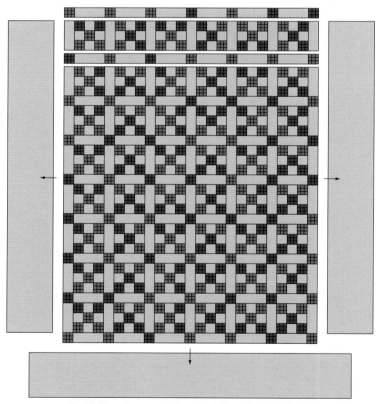

Quilt Top Construction, Adding the Borders

MARKING THE QUILTING PATTERN

A commercial stencil was used to mark the quilt border.

PERSONALIZING YOUR QUILT

Decide how you want to personalize your quilt as part of the border design. Draw a heart on white paper. Then add your own text and floral designs. Finally, trace your finalized design onto the quilt top with a Pigma micron permanent pen. A light box is helpful for this step.

Detail of personalized design

LAYERING

11. Cut the 9 yards of backing into three 3-yard lengths. Remove the selvage and use a ½" seam to sew the three lengths together. Press the backing seams open. After measuring the quilt top, trim the backing so it is about 3" larger than the quilt top on all four sides.

12. Cut the batting about 3" larger than the quilt top on all four sides.

13. Baste all three layers together in preparation for quilting. Refer to page 81 for more detailed instructions.

QUILTING

14. Quilt diagonally every 2" in both directions, through the centers of all the Nine-Patch blocks, over the interior of the quilt top. Quilt the border along the marked lines.

BINDING

15. Cut eleven strips of light background fabric 2¼" by the width of the fabric. Sew them together into one long strip. Fold the entire length of the strip in half lengthwise and press. Attach to the raw edge of the quilt and finish sewing the binding by hand onto the back of the quilt. Refer to page 23 for detailed instructions.

16. Sign and date the back of your quilt. Your wedding quilt is finished!

Choosing a reflective theme creates a relaxing setting for the wedding party's rehearsal dinner.

Your Special Day Is Here

The church is reserved, caterer booked, flowers ordered, and the calendar is down to the final day: the time for your wedding has arrived. In the midst of the fuss and anxious planning, the rehearsal dinner provides an opportunity to prepare for the exciting day ahead in the comfortable company of loved ones.

The rehearsal dinner, as well, can reflect the chosen theme of the wedding. Pictorial displays of the bride and groom's childhood and their courtship are a perfect way to rediscover memories and special events.

"Remember When?..." Collages *Designed by Amy*

A picture collage adds great joy and a time for fun reflection at the rehearsal dinner. Make three separate collages to show the bride during her youth, the groom during his youth, and the couple during their lives together. Purchased ready-made frames placed on individual easels hold the three photograph presentations. To protect the photos, do not use tape or glue, simply arrange photos on the backing board that comes with the frame and cover with the glass. Secure the collage into the frame so the photos will not slip in the frame. A sentimental walk down memory lane, the collages are sure to spark light-hearted conversation and set the wedding party at ease.

Fun for family and friends, display picture collages.

Miniature bags are darling and one-of-a-kind accessories for any dress.

Crazy Quilt Necklace Bag
Designed by Ninette Gehle

SUPPLIES

8¼" x 4½" crazy quilt piece

8¼" x 4½" fabric piece for lining

1½ yards twisted rayon cord

½ yard fold-over decorative trim

Vintage button

INSTRUCTIONS

1. Using a ¼" seam allowance, sew the quilt piece to the lining fabric piece right sides together, leaving an opening for turning. Turn right side out, press, and slipstitch the opening closed.

2. With the lining facing up and the short ends at the top and bottom, fold the bottom edge up 3" to form the bag. Slipstitch the sides of the bag together.

3. Hand sew fold-over trim covering the top edge of the bag. Hand sew the trim along the sides of the bag.

4. Fold the top of the bag down to form the flap.

5. Sew a loop of thread to the center edge of the flap. Sew a button to the bag below the loop.

6. Knot the cord ends and sew the cord ends to the bag at the top sides.

Cranberry Velvet Necklace Bag

Designed by Ninette Gehle

(Photo page 74)

INSTRUCTIONS

1. Using a ¼" seam allowance, sew velvet and lining pieces right sides together, leaving an opening for turning. Turn right side out and sew the opening closed.

2. With the lining facing up and the short ends at the top and bottom, fold the bottom edge up 3" to form the bag.

3. Use embroidery floss to buttonhole stitch (page 114) the side edges together.

4. Fold the top edge down for the flap. Sew a button to the center edge of the flap.

5. For the closure, sew the ball of the snap inside the flap and the socket to the bag.

6. Knot the cord ends; sew the knots to the bag at the top sides. Sew one gold bead and one seed bead to each knot.

SUPPLIES

One 3" x 7½" piece each of velvet and lining fabric
Embroidery floss
1⅛ yards braided rayon cord
Vintage button or jewelry piece
2 gold beads and 2 seed beads
Snap

Tapestry Necklace Bag

Designed by Ninette Gehle

(Photo page 74)

INSTRUCTIONS

1. Using a ¼" seam allowance, sew the tapestry and lining pieces right sides together, leaving an opening for turning. Turn right side out and sew the opening closed.

2. With the short ends at the top and bottom and the lining facing up, fold the bottom edge up 2¼" to form the bag.

3. Use embroidery floss to buttonhole stitch (page 114) the side edges together.

4. Sew trim along the edge of the flap. Sew flat and round beads to the trim.

5. String round and seed beads together onto a threaded needle for 1"; secure the last seed bead by passing the needle back through the previous beads and knotting the thread ends. Repeat to make two more bead dangles. Sew the dangles to the center flap edge.

6. For the closure, sew the ball of the snap inside the flap and the socket to the bag.

7. Fold the ends of the braid up about 1" and knot to secure the ends. Sew the knots of braid to the bag at the top sides.

SUPPLIES

One 3¼" x 6½" piece each of tapestry fabric and lining fabric
Embroidery floss
3" decorative trim
1¼ yards ⅛" flat braid
Assorted seed, round, and flat beads
Snap

Rehearsal Dinner Shoulder Bag

Designed by Ninette Geble

(Photo page 74)

SUPPLIES

5½" x 14" piece each of tapestry fabric for bag and lining fabric

Embroidery floss

⅝ yard ⅛" trim

1⅔ yards twisted rayon cord

Assorted beads, charms, and vintage jewelry

3" tassel

Fabric chalk

Tracing paper

INSTRUCTIONS

1. Trace the curve pattern for the flap onto tracing paper; cut out.

2. Pin fabric and lining right sides together. Use chalk to draw along the curve of the flap template at one end of the pinned fabrics. Sewing along the drawn line and ¼" from edges on the remaining sides, sew the fabrics together, leaving an opening for turning. Turn right side out, press, and hand sew the opening closed.

3. With the lining facing up and the flap at the top, fold the bottom edge up 5" to form the bag.

4. Use floss to buttonhole stitch (page 114) the sides of the bag together and stitch the additional decorative stitches (see Embroidery, beginning on page 114) on the outside of the bag.

5. Sew trim, beads, and jewelry to the flap and the bag as desired. Sew the tassel to the center edge of the flap.

6. Knot the cord ends and sew them to the bag at the top sides.

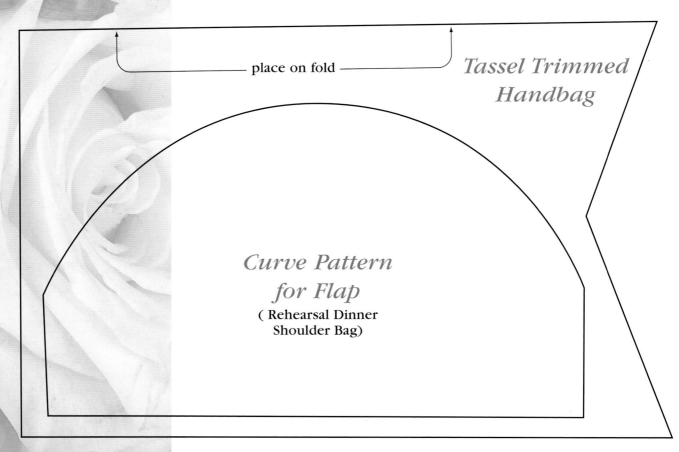

place on fold

Tassel Trimmed Handbag

Curve Pattern for Flap

(Rehearsal Dinner Shoulder Bag)

Tassel Trimmed Handbag

Designed by Ninette Gehle

Vintage fabric, old pieces of jewelry, and trims were used to make this creative and functional handbag.

INSTRUCTIONS

1. Trace the bag pattern (page 76) onto tracing paper; cut out.

2. Fold each fabric square in half. Use the template to cut one shape from each bag fabric and lining fabric.

3. With right sides together and using a ¼" seam, sew the bag shape along the short straight edge (center back seam). Matching angled edges (bottom) and centering the seam at the back, sew the bottom of bag. Repeat to sew the lining, leaving an opening in the bottom seam for turning the bag later.

4. Matching the right sides and top edges of the bag and lining, sew together ¼" from the top edges. Turn bag right side out. Slipstitch the opening closed and insert the lining into the bag.

5. Press the ends of tassel trim ¼" to the wrong side. Hand sew trim along the front bottom edge. Hand sew one button to center of trim.

6. Hand sew rickrack around the top edge of the bag.

7. String two pearl beads and three gold beads onto a threaded needle, stringing a small bead last. Pass the needle back through the previous beads to secure; knot the thread ends. Sew the bead dangle to the center top of the bag. Sew a button above the bead dangle.

8. Cut the ribbon in half. Knot the ribbons together about 1" from each end. Sew the knots to the bag at each side.

9. String three beads onto a threaded needle, stringing a small bead last; pass the needle back through the previous beads to secure. Sew to one knot of the ribbon handle. Repeat for the other knot.

SUPPLIES

- 10" square each of fabric for bag and lining fabric
- ¼ yard rickrack
- 5" of ½" decorative tassel trim
- ¾ yard ⅛" satin ribbon
- Assorted vintage beads and jewels
- Tracing paper

Debbie's Wedding Quilt, Ann Boyce, quilted by Terry Ballard, 84¹/2" X 84¹/2", sixty-four 9¹/2" finished blocks.

Debbie's Wedding Quilt

Note from the designer, Ann Boyce:

After our friend Debbie Driscoll arrived at the Fall International Quilt Market in Houston with a gorgeous diamond engagement ring, Marinda Stewart, Luella Doss and I collaborated to make Debbie a surprise wedding quilt. Donna Wilder told us that Debbie had a new condominium decorated in a neutral color scheme. I pieced the front of the quilt with thirty different neutral fabrics. We cut up rectangles for the pieced backing and mailed them to everyone we could think of in the quilt industry for signatures. By spring it was finished. When we presented the quilt to Debbie at the Spring International Quilt Market in St. Louis, she cried. This was her first quilt! This quilt would be perfect to present at the rehearsal dinner.

INSTRUCTIONS

CUTTING

SIGNATURE STRIPS: Cut two 2½" strips from each of twenty-five fabrics. Cut the strips into 2½" x 10" rectangles. (Mail more signature strips than needed in case some are not returned. If you run short, fill in with blank strips. This quilt requires 185 signature strips.)

BLOCKS

Cut one 3⅞" strip from each of the thirty fabrics. Cut the strips into 256 3⅞" squares (8 or 9 per strip). Cut the squares in half diagonally (512 A triangles).

Cut two 2¼" strips from each of twenty-three fabrics and four 2¼" strips from each of seven fabrics. Cut the strips into 512 2¼" x 5⅝" rectangles (7 per strip). Cut off one end at 45° using a rotary cutting ruler with a 45° angle (512 B pieces).

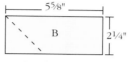

Cut 45° angle.

BLOCK ASSEMBLY

Use ¼" seam allowance unless otherwise stated.

1. Stitch an A triangle to a B piece. Repeat to make 512 triangle units. Press.

Sew A to B.

Stitch to make a square unit.

2. Stitch two triangle units together to make a square unit. Press. Repeat to make 256 square units.

3. Stitch four square units together to make a block. Press. Repeat to make 64 blocks.

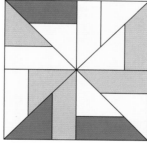

Stitch to make the block.

QUILT ASSEMBLY

4. Arrange the blocks on a table, floor, or design wall in horizontal rows.

5. Sew the blocks into rows. Press the seams of row 1 to the right. Press the seams of row 2 to the left. Continue until all eight rows are sewn. Alternate the pressing direction from one row to the next so the seams will lay flat when sewing the rows together.

6. Sew the rows together. Then press the top completely.

BORDERS

7. Measure the quilt from top to bottom across the middle. Cut two borders parallel to the selvage 4½" wide by the length of the quilt. Pin and sew the borders onto the sides. Press. If you have a walking foot for your machine, this is a good time to use it, as it will keep the fabrics from stretching.

SUPPLIES

½ yard each of 30 neutral fabrics for quilt top and signature backing strips (Cut first and mail.)

2½ yards for border and binding (Cut strips parallel to selvage.)

1 yard neutral fabric for backing sashing

2½ yards neutral fabric for backing border (Cut strips parallel to selvage.)

89" x 89" batting

Gold metallic thread for machine quilting

8. Measure the quilt from side to side across the middle. Cut two borders parallel to the selvage 4½" wide by the width of the quilt. Pin and sew the borders onto the top and bottom. Press.

9. Press the quilt top well.

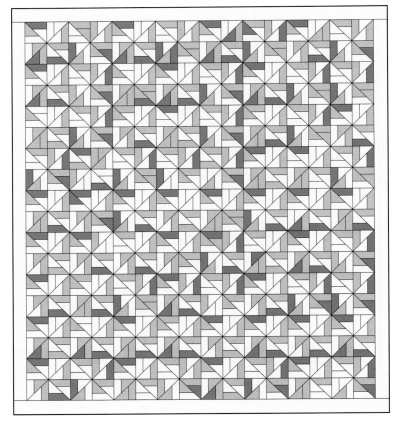

Quilt top construction

BACKING

10. Sew the signature strips together in five columns of thirty-seven strips each. Press seams open.

11. Cut two 2" strips of backing sashing fabric. Stitch together to make one long length. Repeat seven times for a total of eight sashing strips. Measure the columns of signature strips from top to bottom across the middle and determine the average length. Trim six sashing strips this length and sew them between and on each side of the columns of signature strips. Press toward sashing strips. Measure the width of this piece from side to side across the middle and trim the remaining two sashing strips to this length. Sew to the top and bottom. Press toward sashing strips.

12. Cut two 6" strips from the backing border fabric parallel to the selvage. Stitch together to make one long length. Repeat one more time. Measure the backing from side to side across the middle and trim the strips to this length. Stitch to the top and bottom of the backing. Press toward borders.

13. Cut two 16" strips from the backing border fabric parallel to the selvage. Stitch together to make one long length. Repeat one more time. Measure the backing from top to bottom across the middle and trim the strips to this length. Stitch to the sides of the backing. Press towards borders.

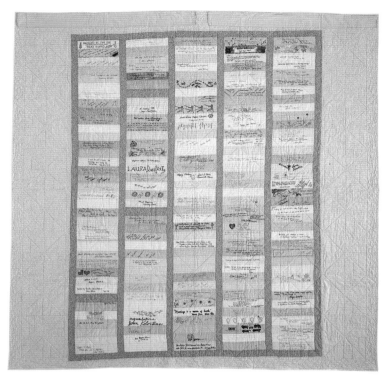

Signature quilt back

LAYERING

14. You are now ready to sandwich your quilt top, batting and backing fabrics together to make the quilt. Spread the pieced backing fabric, wrong side up, onto large tables or a hard floor. Tape the edges down with masking tape. Layer the batting on the backing fabric. Place the quilt top on top of the batting and backing, centering it. Now pin baste or hand baste the layers together. The basting should be at least 3" apart, any larger and you may get puckers on the back. When you are finished basting, you can remove the tape and lift the quilt off the surface. You are ready to quilt.

QUILTING

15. This quilt was machine quilted in-the-ditch around each piece of the blocks with gold metallic thread. A continuous line heart motif was machine quilted in the border.

BINDING

Cut four 2¼"-wide binding strips parallel to the selvage. Sew them together into one long strip. Fold the entire length of the strip in half lengthwise and press. Sew the binding to the raw edge of the quilt and finish by hand sewing the binding onto the back of the quilt. Refer to page 23 for more detailed instructions.

Now Debbie is happily married and this beautiful quilt decorates their new home in South Carolina.

The Celebration

No time is more special than the occasion of a wedding. The extra steps taken to make the event resound with the wedding couple's personalities create the most memorable "snap shots" taken away by those in attendance.

A Day To Remember

A memorable wedding celebration is one that transforms ordinary traditions into expressions of personal style. Even the simplest projects can make incredible wedding impressions. For instance, the dramatic effect of the guests' first approach to beautiful doors clad in large grapevine wreaths with flowing ribbons is a magnificent way to start the celebration. Simple details throughout the ceremony that serve function and beauty are easy to incorporate into the wedding. Romantic vintage lace and linens make excellent accents for a guest book or a traditional ring bearer's pillow. For a novel approach, a bubbly send-off for the newly married couple is a wedding activity that is quickly becoming a tradition. Whatever your needs, you will find the projects in this section present several unique wedding accessories and ideas to create a glorious wedding event.

Wedding Wreaths

Designed by Mildred Conrad and Donna Martin

The marriage of a son or daughter is a very special time for family and friends to gather. Welcome your guests with wreaths at the ceremony entrances. Wreaths can be placed on either the inside or outside of a door. Here, we chose two large grapevine wreaths to accent the outside of bold church doors. Lovely ribbons and flowers are coordinating touches, adding color and dimension, and setting the stage for the celebration to come.

Beautiful wreaths start off the wedding celebration.

SUPPLIES

(for 2 wreaths)

Two 30" diameter grapevine
   wreaths
1 bunch of twigs
11 yards 4" wired pink ombré
   French silk ribbon
14 yards 1½" ivory satin or
   brocade bridal ribbon
18 yards 4" ivory toile ribbon
22 gauge floral wire
The following artificial or
   fresh flowers:
      12-16 large flowers
      20-24 medium flowers
      24-28 small flowers
      12-16 baby's breath sprays
Wire cutters
Hot glue gun and glue sticks, if
   needed

INSTRUCTIONS

Note: Follow all steps to make each wreath. Hang wreaths on the wall for ease of assembly. Use half of each ribbon length to make each bow on each wreath. Because your flower selection may differ from ours, work for an overall pleasing visual arrangement when placing flowers into wreath.

1. Begin by inserting extra twigs into the wreath at one side to give additional dimension to the design.

Insert extra twigs.

2. For bows, follow Making a Floral Bow (page 113) to make one bow with 24" streamers from each silk, bridal, and toile ribbons.

3. Wire toile bow, bridal bow, and finally, silk bow to the side of the wreath with extra twigs. Intermingle loops of the bows to create one beautiful bow.

4. Insert larger flowers close to the bow and add smaller flowers working away from the bow. Insert baby's breath among all the flowers.

Vintage lace and silk ribbon embroidery are special additions to the cover of an ordinary purchased guest book.

Special Guest Book
Designed by Mildred Conrad and Donna Martin

INSTRUCTIONS

1. Use a running stitch to gather the straight edge of the bridal lace into a circle, overlapping the lace ends.

Gather lace into a circle.

SUPPLIES

Brocade fabric-covered
  guest book
14" of 2" bridal lace trim
2½" x 3" motif cut from
  vintage lace or a purchased
  lace appliqué
4mm pink silk ribbon
4mm green silk ribbon
Assorted pearls
5 pearl sprays
Craft glue

2. Glue the center of the lace circle to one corner of the book, weighting with a heavy object until dry if necessary.

3. Glue the ends of the pearl sprays under the lace circle.

4. Refer to the illustration below and follow Silk Ribbon Embroidery (beginning on page 115) to stitch pink spider web roses and green lazy daisy leaves on the lace motif or appliqué. Glue pearls to the laces.

5. Glue embellished laces to the lace circle on the book.

Designed by
Donna Martin

(Photo page 85)

INSTRUCTIONS

1. Cut the stems of the flowers and leaves to about 8" to 10" long.

2. Place the stems next to pen about halfway up from the pen point. Use florist tape to wrap the stems and pen together, covering all of the pen except the area close to the point.

3. Tie the ribbon into a bow around the pen; trim the ribbon ends. Glue the bow in place to secure.

SUPPLIES

Ball point pen without pocket clip
⅝ yard 1½" French silk wired ribbon
Silk or dried flowers and leaves
Green florist tape
Hot glue gun and glue sticks

Perfect Programs

The wedding program is one detail that should not be omitted. A program informs wedding guests and becomes an invaluable written record of the ceremony. A basic tri-folded linen-paper program with elegant lettering is an easy document to design on a personal computer. A professional printer can also create and fold all of your programs. For a formal touch, present a book-style program with pages tied together with romantic tulle ribbon threaded through two holes punched at the top of layered pages.

Program content should include: a ceremony outline and listing of parents, the wedding party, other attendants, participants, and officiants. This is also an appropriate space to acknowledge friends and special family members or offer an endearing sentiment such as a favorite poem shared by the wedding couple. After the wedding day, this record should be tucked away with other cherished wedding mementos.

The Marriage of
Amy Melissa Martin
and
Robert John Barickman II

The Marriage Celebration
of
Lynne Paige Garner
and
Christian Charles McElhinney

Saturday, September 16, 1995
6:00 pm
Central Presbyterian Church
Des Moines, Iowa

An elegant program with script writing and tulle bow at top

Heart Ring Bearer's Pillow
Designed by Ninette Gehle

INSTRUCTIONS

1. Trace the pattern (page 89) twice onto tracing paper for templates; cut out. Cut one template in half horizontally for the pillow back.

2. For the pillow front, fold the taffeta square in half. Match the fold line of whole template to the fold of the fabric and cut out the heart shape.

Pearls, lace, and ribbon enhance a simple heart shape to make a wonderful ring bearer's pillow.

SUPPLIES

14" square ivory moiré taffeta
14" square of ivory satin
7/8 yard 4 1/2" double-edged ivory lace
1/2 yard 3/4" ivory flat lace
Ivory satin ribbons:
   14" of 1 5/8"
   1/3 yard of 2 1/4"
   Two 1-yard lengths of 5/8"
   1 yard of 1/8"
Assorted round and iris pearls, and mother of pearl, crystal, and seed beads
Polyester fiber fill
Tracing paper

3. For the pillow back, fold the satin square in half. Leaving at least ½" between the top and bottom halves of the cut-apart template, match the fold lines for each template to the fold of fabric. Allowing ¼" for seam allowance at each edge where the templates were cut apart, cut out the shapes.

4. With right sides together, sew the straight edges of the top and bottom halves together, leaving a 3" section at center unsewn. Press the seam open.

5. Sew the pillow front to the pillow back with right sides together; clip curves, turn right side out, and press.

6. Stuff the pillow with fiber fill; sew the opening closed.

7. For the hand loop at the back of pillow, cut a 5½" length from 1⅝"-wide ribbon. Press the ends ¼" to the wrong side. Center the ribbon over the back seam and stitch the ends to the pillow.

8. For the front embellishment, sew the ends of 4½"-wide lace together. Use a running stitch along one edge to gather the lace into a circle; knot the thread. Hand sew the lace circle to the center front of the pillow.

9. Form each remaining 2¼" and 1⅝" satin ribbon into loops by bringing each ribbon's ends to the center and stitching together. Stack the ribbon loops and tie the remaining ⅝" and ⅛" ribbons and the lace trim around the centers of the loops to form a bow. Knot and trim the ends of the ribbon and lace.

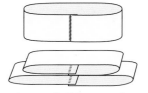

Form loops of ribbon and stack.

10. For the bead dangle, string one iris bead and two pearls onto a threaded needle; repeat two or three times. Continue to string one pearl, one crystal bead, one pearl again, one mother-of-pearl bead, and one seed bead. Insert the needle back through the beads and tie off at the top to secure. Sew the bead dangle to the center of the bow. Repeat for the second bead dangle.

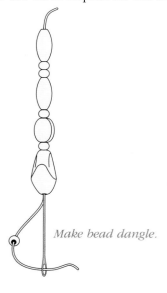

Make bead dangle.

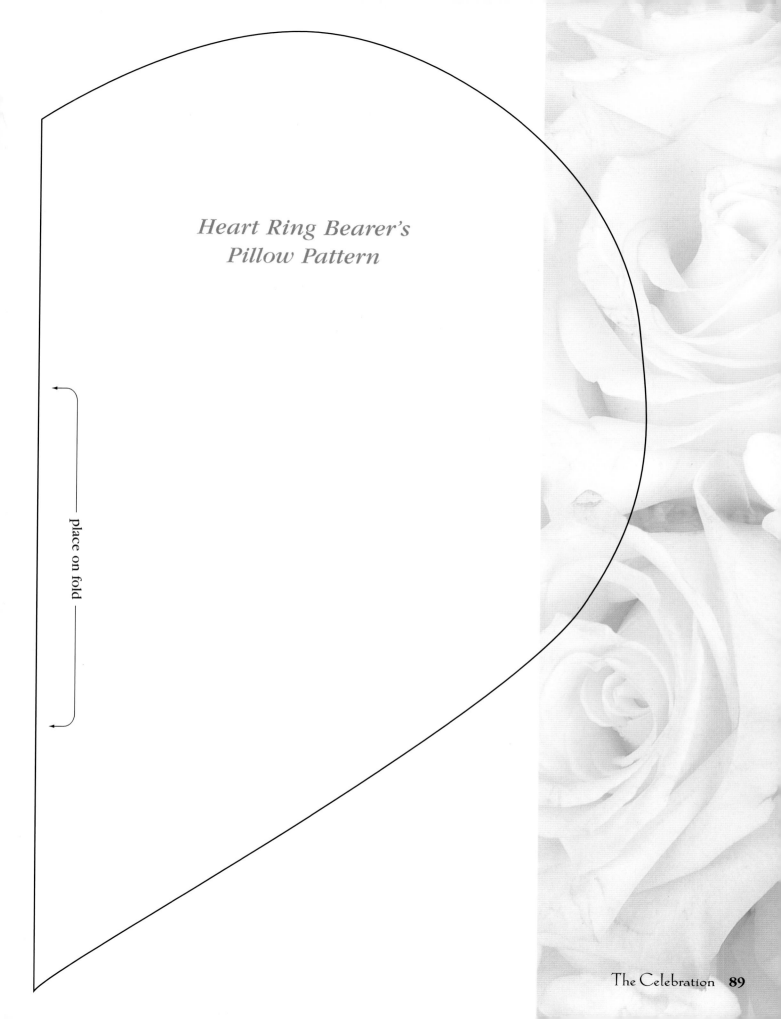

Heart Ring Bearer's Pillow Pattern

place on fold

Iridescent seed beads and pearls are romantic pretties against an heirloom handkerchief.

Handkerchief Ring Bearer's Cushion

Designed by Ninette Gehle

SUPPLIES

10"- to 12"-square vintage handkerchief with a 3" lace border

Two 5½" ivory fabric squares
for under pillow

Polyester fiber fill

5½" of 2¼" ivory satin ribbon

5 yards ⅛" ivory satin ribbon

¾ yard ¾" ivory flat lace

⅔ yard 1¼" ivory motif lace
trim

Assorted round and iris pearls,
crystal beads, and seed beads

3 ivory ribbon roses

INSTRUCTIONS

1. For the under pillow, sew the fabric squares right sides together, leaving an opening for turning. Turn right side out, stuff with fiber fill, and sew the opening closed. For the hand loop on the back of the pillow, press ¼" of each end of the 2¼"-wide ribbon to the wrong side, center the ribbon on the back of the pillow, and hand sew the ends to the pillow.

2. Cut one ½-yard length from each flat lace and motif lace. Hand sew the motif lace along one edge of the flat lace. Use a running stitch to gather the remaining lace edge into a circle; knot and trim the thread. Hand sew the lace circle to the center of the handkerchief. Gather the remaining flat lace length into a small circle and hand sew to the center of the large lace circle.

3. For the ribbon streamers, cut the ⅛" ribbon into six equal lengths. Varying the lengths of each bow streamer, tie the ribbons into bows with small loops. Sew the bows to the center of the lace circle. For each streamer end, form a loop about 1" from end and knot to secure. String one larger bead or pearl and one seed bead onto a threaded needle and sew the beads to each ribbon knot.

4. Sew ribbon roses over the bow loops at the center of the handkerchief.

5. Cut four motifs from the remaining motif lace and hand sew one motif to each corner of the handkerchief.

6. Sew pearls and beads to the laces and handkerchief.

7. Place the handkerchief over the pillow, offsetting corners; tack in place.

Dainty Flower Girl Barrette

Designed by Margaret Cox

Silk and sheer ribbons were used to create a rosette hair barrette for the flower girl.

INSTRUCTIONS

1. Fold sheer ribbon in half lengthwise. Twist the wires together at one end and pull the wires at the opposite end to gather the ribbon to fit around the outer edge of the barrette. Glue the gathered edges of the folded ribbon around the outer edge of the barrette.

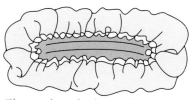

Glue gathered edges to barrette.

2. Follow Making Ribbon Flowers and Leaves: Crushed Rose and Folded Leaf (pages 119 and 122) to make a rosebud from variegated ribbon and two leaves from green ribbon. Glue the rosebud and leaves to top of barrette.

SUPPLIES

½ yard 1½" sheer wired ribbon
⅓ yard 1½" green silk wired ribbon
⅓ yard 1" pink-and-yellow variegated silk wired ribbon
Craft hair barrette
Hot glue gun and glue sticks

SUPPLIES

Wicker basket

1 yard ivory twisted decorative cord

1/3 yard 1" ivory ombré satin wired ribbon

1½ yards 1" pink-and-yellow variegated silk wired ribbon

1½ yards 1½" green silk wired ribbon

Pearl stamens

Ivory acrylic spray paint

Gold acrylic paint

Small sponge pieces

Hot glue gun and glue sticks

Ribbon Flower Key

Half Primrose with stem and calyx
ivory and green ribbon

Crushed Rose
pink-and-yellow variegated ribbon

Crushed Rosebud
pink-and-yellow variegated ribbon

Folded Leaf
green ribbon

Gathered Leaf
green ribbon

Flower Girl Basket

Designed by
Margaret Cox

A simple wicker basket can be transformed into a beautiful wedding-day accent with elegant trims and wired ribbon.

INSTRUCTIONS

1. If necessary, cut the existing handles from the basket at the rim.

2. Spray paint the basket ivory. Use sponges to lightly paint the rim and lower edge of basket gold; wipe off the excess paint.

3. Cut cord length in half. Knot the cords together at the centers. Glue the ends to the inside top edge of the basket to form a handle.

4. Refer to the illustration below and Ribbon Flower Key, and follow Making Ribbon Flowers and Leaves (beginning on page 118) to make flowers and leaves from ribbons.

5. Arrange flowers and leaves on one side of the basket; hot glue in place, pushing the flowers and leaves flat against the basket.

Design placement

Woven Cardholders

Designed by Ninette Gehle

INSTRUCTIONS

Note: Sew ¼" seams with fabric right sides together unless otherwise stated. For an alternate look, add a ruffle and embellish with tassel trim, pearls, and a twisted rayon handle.

1. Cut six 7½" lengths from light-colored ribbon and seven 6½" lengths from darker-colored ribbon.

2. Cut four 6½" x 7½" pieces from fabric for lining.

A woven ribbon bag for gift cards is accented by a beaded silver wire pouch designed by Susan Christie.

3. Place one fabric piece wrong side up. Place the darker colored ribbon lengths across the fabric piece; pin the ends in place. Pin one end of each light-colored ribbon length along the top of the fabric. Weave light-colored ribbons over and behind the pinned darker colored ribbons.

4. Sew the ends of the ribbon to the fabric to secure the weave.

5. Match the right side of one fabric piece to the ribbon side of the woven piece and sew along the sides and bottom to form the bag. Turn right side out.

6. Optional: For a ruffle, meet the short ends of the fabric strip and sew the ends together to form a ring. Meeting the long edges and wrong sides, fold the ring in half. Use a running stitch along the raw edges to gather the ring to fit around the bag opening. Match the raw edges of ruffle to the raw edge of bag; adjust the gathers and baste in place.

7. For the lining, sew the remaining two fabric pieces together along the long edges. Press one short edge (bottom) ¼" to the wrong side.

8. Matching the raw edges and side seams at the top, slip the woven bag into the lining tube. Sew the lining to the bag.

9. Turn the lining up over the bag. Hand sew the bottom of lining closed and insert the lining into the bag.

10. Sew the decorative trim along the top of the front of the bag. Sew ribbon roses to the trim and attach an antique jewelry piece, or sew pearls to the decorative trim.

11. For the handles, cut ribbon or twisted cord in half; knot each end. Sew the knots of one cord length to the front below the ruffle; repeat for the back.

SUPPLIES

1⅓ yards each of 1" light- and darker-colored ribbons

¼ yard fabric for lining

3" x 20" light-colored rayon fabric strip for ruffle (optional)

1 yard twisted rayon cord or narrow ribbon for handles

7" decorative trim

5 ribbon roses

Antique jewelry pieces or assorted pearls

Bubbles, Bubbles...

Blowing bubbles as the couple leaves the wedding event is a relatively new idea and one that does not cause distress to church or hotel grounds. On a beautiful day, lofty bubbles create a glorious look which is then reflected in wedding-day photographs—times never to be forgotten. You

What a fun alternative to birdseed or rice.

can purchase small bottles, decorated and ready for use. However, larger bottles of bubbles purchased at a discount store are more economical and can be disguised in special packaging, in this case, clever fabric wraps. We chose floral print fabric, and cut it into 4" squares that were gathered around each bottle and secured with a rubber band. A ribbon bow hides the thrifty construction. Silk flowers can also be glued to the top or tucked under the ribbon. Arranged in large baskets decorated with silk flowers and ribbons, the bubble bottles are easy for attendants to distribute as guests leave the ceremony.

Bubbles, bubbles everywhere!

Christi and Ed's Memories, Nicki Jean, 58" x 64",
seventy-two 6" finished Rail Fence blocks.

Christi and Ed's Memories Quilt

Note from the designer, Nicki Jean:

The idea for making the quilt came from a group discussion at a Valley Quilt Guild meeting. Since I had already made retirement and thank you quilts, I knew creating a quilt for Christi and Ed would make their day extra special. I made this quilt for my daughter and son-in-law so they would have a lasting memory of the people who attended their wedding. This particular block was chosen for two reasons: it was quick and easy; and I had 2½" 100% cotton scraps from several Log Cabin quilts I had made. I ironed freezer paper to the back side of the white strip to make the fabric stiffer, and thus easier to sign. The blocks were placed in a basket at the reception and made available for the guests to sign with a Pigma micron permanent pen. I then finished the quilt and presented it to the couple at a later date. This quilt could also be completed before the wedding day and signed at the reception.

SUPPLIES

The following gives you the total yardage needed, assuming the fabric is at least 42" wide.

¼ yard each of 14 different medium and dark fabrics for the dark rails

1 yard of white-on-white print for the white signature rails

⅜ yard of dark fabric for the inner border

1½ yards of print fabric for the outer border and binding

Backing: 4 yards

Batting: 62" x 68"

Pigma micron permanent pen

Embroidery floss to tie the quilt

INSTRUCTIONS

Rail Fence Blocks

CUTTING

Medium and dark rails: Cut two 2½"-wide strips across the width of each fabric.

White-on-white rails: Cut twelve 2½"-wide strips across the width of the fabric.

BLOCK ASSEMBLY

1. Sew two strips from each medium or dark fabric (one on each side) onto one white strip. It should measure 6½" wide. Press as the arrows indicate.

2. Trim the left end straight.

3. Cut the sewn strips into 6½" blocks.

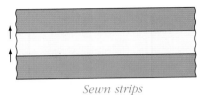

Sewn strips

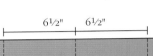

6½" blocks

QUILT ASSEMBLY

4. Lay out your blocks as shown.

5. Sew the blocks into rows and then sew the rows together.

Quilt top construction

INNER BORDER

6. Cut six 1½" strips across the width of the fabric. Sew the strips together into one continuous strip.

7. Measure the width of the quilt across the middle. Cut two strips this measurement. Pin and sew the borders onto the top and bottom.

8. Measure the length of the quilt across the middle. Cut two strips this measurement. Pin and sew the borders onto each side.

OUTER BORDER

9. Cut six 4½" strips across the width of the fabric. Sew the strips together into one continuous strip.

10. Measure the width of the quilt across the middle. Cut two strips this measurement. Pin and sew the borders onto the top and bottom.

11. Measure the length of the quilt across the middle. Cut two strips this measurement. Pin and sew the borders onto each side.

12. Press the quilt top well.

LAYERING AND TIEING

13. Cut the 4 yards of backing into two 2-yard lengths. Remove the selvages and use a ½" seam allowance to sew the two lengths together. Press the backing seam open. After measuring the quilt top, trim the backing so it is 2-3" larger than the quilt top on all four sides.

14. Cut the batting about 2-3" larger than the quilt top on all four sides.

15. Layer the backing (wrong side up), the batting, and the quilt top (right side up). Refer to page 81 for more detailed instructions.

16. Tie the quilt at the block intersections with the knots on the top. Trim the batting and backing even with the quilt top.

BINDING

17. Cut seven strips of binding fabric 2¼" by the width of the fabric. Sew them together into one long strip. Fold the entire length of the strip in half lengthwise and press. Attach the raw edge to the quilt and finish sewing the binding by hand onto the back of the quilt. Refer to page 23 for more detailed instructions.

This is a quilt the happy couple will enjoy in the years to come.

Sew Trousseau

*Romantic garments and accessories for the bride become treasured keepsakes
holding a special place in her heart.*

Beribboned and Beautiful

Acquiring the trousseau is an exciting aspect of the bride's wedding experience. The garments and accessories adorned with antique frilly laces, sewn-on pearls, and blooming silk ribbon embroidery stitches and the quilt in this section are loving touches for any bridal trousseau. Included are a sweet T-shirt with an added-on lace vest and lovely sweater sets with spring flowers worked in colorful silk ribbon. For honeymoon travel, elegant jewelry cases of taffeta embellished with beaded lace are perfect stowaways and also make wonderful personal gifts.

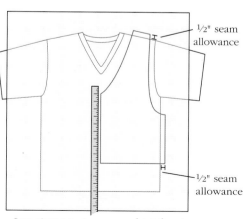

Lacy Vested Tee

Designed by Amy

An ordinary T-shirt becomes a romantic blouse with a few touches of lace, ribbon, and a sewn-on charm.

INSTRUCTIONS

1. For the lace vest overlay pattern, lay tissue paper over the front of the shirt. Referring to the illustration, use a ruler to draw a vertical line marking the center front and to draw the desired right vest shape on the tissue paper. Cut out the pattern adding 1/2" to the armhole, neck, center front, and lower edges. Use the pattern to cut the vest fronts from lace (reversing pattern for left front).

1/2" seam allowance

1/2" seam allowance

Lay tissue paper over shirt front and draw vest shape.

SUPPLIES
Ivory V-necked T-shirt
5/8 yard ivory lace
2 5/8 yards 1/2" ivory lace trim
2 1/2" x 6 1/2" lace V appliqué
2 3/4" x 6" lace appliqué for pocket
3 1/2" diameter lace doily
Serger thread to match T-shirt
1 1/2" heart charm
4mm green silk ribbon and embroidery floss to match
Two ribbon roses
Tissue paper
Hot glue gun and glue sticks

2. For the serged ruffled edges on the T-shirt's neck, sleeves, and lower edges, follow the manufacturer's instructions to set your serger for a narrow ruffled edge. Serge the neck edge. At the lower edge of the shirt, trim the sides to make rounded corners. Serge around the lower edge, trimming away the existing hem. Serge around each sleeve, trimming away the existing hems.

3. Serge (overlock) the armhole, neck, center front, and lower edges of the lace vest shapes. Press these edges ½" to the wrong side and sew in place.

4. For the ties, cut two 8" lengths of lace trim. Sew the end of one lace trim length to the top center front edge of each vest shape.

5. Sew lace V appliqué to the bottom center front corner of the right vest shape.

6. For the left vest shape, pin the remaining appliqué to the lower edge and sew along the short and long bottom edges, forming a pocket. Sew lace trim along the neck, center front, and lower edge of vest.

7. To attach the vest shapes to the shirt, press ½" to wrong side at the shoulders and sides. Pin the vest shapes to the shirt and topstitch the shoulders and sides in place.

8. Sew the doily below the neck; sew a charm at the center of the doily. Glue ribbon roses to the charm. Use green ribbon and floss and follow Silk Ribbon Embroidery: French Knot Couched Bow (page 118) to make the bow above the charm.

If you do not have a serger to make ruffled edges on a T-shirt, there are a variety of techniques you can use for creative edge finishes. Try sewing or gluing lace trims, pearl edging, or narrow ribbon to the neckline or around the sleeve edges. If you have a sewing machine that sews decorative stitches, utilize a pretty stitch motif to add flare to your shirt. Even an ordinary zigzag sewn with decorative embroidery thread can make a regular shirt something special.

Come live with me, and be my love,
And we will some new pleasures prove
Of golden sands, and crystal brooks,
With silken lines, and silver hooks.

—John Donne
The Bait, Stanza I

Taffeta Jewelry Case

Designed by Ninette Gehle

INSTRUCTIONS

Note: Sew ¼" seams with fabric right sides together unless otherwise stated.

1. For each pocket flap, meet the long edges and right sides of each fabric piece and sew the raw edges together, leaving a small opening for turning. Turn the flaps right side out and press; slipstitch the openings closed. Set the flaps aside.

2. To hem each pocket, press one short edge (top) of the pocket fabric piece ¼" to the wrong side; press again 1". Sew the medium and small pocket hems close to the first pressed edge. Embroider herringbone stitch (page 114) across the front of the large pocket, catching the hem in the stitching.

An elegant jewelry case made from soft hues of silk and taffeta accented with lace and heirloom embroidery is a wonderful gift for the bride.

3. To assemble the pockets, pin the small pocket to the medium pocket, right sides up and matching the lower edges. Stitching through all layers, embroider stem stitch (page 115) on the small pocket 2½" from each side to divide the small pocket piece into three pockets.

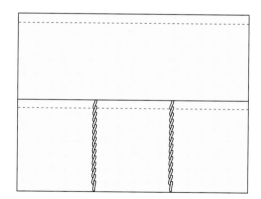

Pin small pocket to medium pocket and stitch to divide into three pockets.

4. Sewing through all the layers, sew the seamed long edge of one flap above the divided small pockets. Press the flap down over the small pockets and embroider stem stitch (page 115) across flap close to the top edge.

5. With right sides up, pin the medium/small pocket unit to the large pocket. Repeat Step 4 to sew the remaining flap above the medium pocket.

SUPPLIES

8½" x 12½" piece of moiré taffeta

Pieces of silky fabric:
   8½" x 12½" for lining
   8½" x 11¼" for large pocket
   8½" x 7" for medium pocket
   8½" x 4¼" for small pocket
   Two 9" x 4" for pocket flaps

Vintage lace appliqués for front of bag and button closure

2½" of narrow lace trim for closure

Assorted buttons, pearls, and beads

Embroidery floss to match taffeta

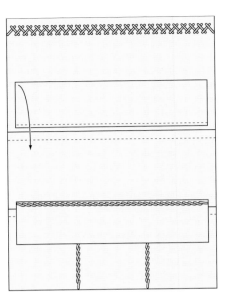

Pin medium and small pockets to large pocket and sew flap.

6. With right sides up, match the lower edges and baste the pockets to the lining fabric piece.

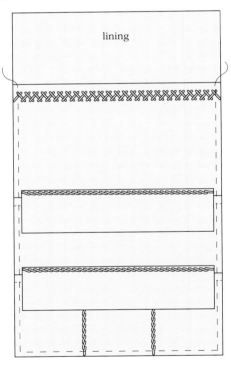

Baste pockets to lining

7. With right sides together, sew the taffeta fabric piece and lining together, leaving an opening for turning at the top edge. Turn the jewelry case right side out and press. Hand sew the opening closed.

8. Sew lace appliqué(s) to the front of the bag. Sew pearls and beads to the lace. Sew a button to the bag at the center of the front edge. Using the 2½" length of narrow lace trim, form a loop; stitch the ends to the back of the case opposite the button. Sew a small lace appliqué over the ends of the loop.

*Silk ribbon embroidery bouquets embellish
a simple cotton sweater set.*

Green Sweater Set *Designed by Sandy Belt*

INSTRUCTIONS

1. Referring to the illustrations and Stitch Key (page 104), follow Silk Ribbon Embroidery (beginning on page 115) to stitch designs on the cardigan upper left and right fronts and the sweater center front neck edge.

2. Use light blue ribbon to sew buttons to the cardigan, bringing ribbon over the edges of button and down through the center holes.

Lace and Ribbon Sweater Set *Designed by Sandy Belt*

INSTRUCTIONS

1. Measure across one shoulder of cardigan; add 1". Cut two lengths of lace this measurement. Measure along the front neck edge of the sweater; add 1". Cut one length of lace this measurement.

2. Sew the lace to the cardigan shoulders and along the front neck edge of the sweater.

3. Referring to the illustrations and Stitch Key (page 104) as a guide, follow Silk Ribbon Embroidery (beginning on page 115) to stitch designs over the lace on the cardigan shoulders and sweater neckline.

SUPPLIES

Ladies' green cardigan and
  sweater set
1½ yards 4mm ivory silk
  ribbon
2½ yards 4mm light blue
  silk ribbon
2 yards 4mm blue silk ribbon
2½ yards 4mm purple silk
  ribbon
2 yards 4mm green silk ribbon
2½ yards 7mm pink silk
  ribbon
Two ¾" diameter pearl buttons
Two ⅞" diameter pearl buttons

SUPPLIES

Ladies' ivory cardigan and
  sweater set
1"-wide vintage lace for
  cardigan shoulders and
  sweater neck edge
½ yard 4mm ivory silk ribbon
1 yard 4mm yellow silk ribbon
2 yards 4mm variegated pink
  silk ribbon
2 yards 4mm purple silk ribbon
2 yards 4mm light blue silk
  ribbon
2½ yards 4mm green silk
  ribbon

Green Sweater Stitch Key

Ruched Rose
pink

Lazy Daisy Stitch
blue

French Knots
*light blue for
flower centers,
purple for lilacs,
ivory for accent
couching*

**Japanese Ribbon
Stitch**
green

Couching
green

**French Knot
Couching**
green

Ivory Sweater Stitch Key

Japanese Ribbon Stitch
*variegated pink flower
petals*

Lazy Daisy Stitch
*green leaves, yellow
flower petals*

French Knots
*ivory flower centers,
light blue flower clusters*

Couching
green

**Straight Stitch with
French Knot**
purple

*Sweater
center front*

Cardigan left front (reverse for right front)

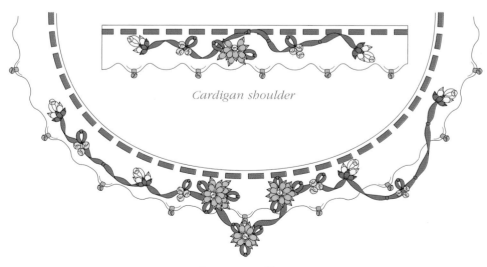

Cardigan shoulder

Sweater neckline

Ocean Waves Quilt, Wendy McGrath, 81" x 94"

Ocean Waves Quilt

Note from the designer, Wendy McGrath:

A neutral scrap quilt is always appropriate for a newly married couple who are just beginning to solidify their individual tastes into a mutually agreeable decorating scheme. The geometry of the ocean waves piecing is cleanly pleasing to anyone who fears a fussy, feminine bedroom quilt. The solid trapunto blocks add a touch of elegant handwork and another dimension to the finished quilt. Yarn creates stuffed areas which rise above the quilting design. This trapunto star design is an adaptation of one designed by Adele Ingraham. Its straight-line design makes the process of threading yarn through the channels quite easy. The trapunto work was done before the ocean wave triangle units were applied. This allows you to cut the trapunto block to an accurate quilt block size after the yarn stuffing.

SUPPLIES

2¼ yards white- or cream-colored top fabric for the trapunto blocks

2¼ yards white batiste, or other lightweight woven fabric suitable for easy puncturing with large-eyed needle threaded with yarn for the under layer of the trapunto blocks

10⅛ yards of a variety of neutral fabrics for the ocean waves triangles (Eighty-one different ⅛ yard pieces would be wonderful, but more or fewer fabrics will work. Using your own fabric stash of neutral scraps for the 2,268 triangles required can substantially lower your yardage needs.)

7½ yards for backing

86" x 99" batting

½ yard for binding

Large-eye yarn needle

4-ply acrylic knitting worsted yarn

FABRIC TIPS

As with any scrap quilt, the more fabrics that are used, the more interesting the quilt becomes. Within the range of neutral, choose fabrics from stark white to light brown. You may want to mix in tans with a touch of rose or a hint of gold and some black prints for emphasis. Use a good variety of print scale from small to large and delicate to bold and floral to geometric. What scrap quilt could do without stripes, plaids, checks, and other needed "line and design" type fabrics? These give a special needed beat to a neutrals quilt, which is by definition restricted in color impact and therefore must pick up interest with contrast in pattern.

INSTRUCTIONS

Trapunto Blocks

The trapunto work should be completed first.

1. Cut twenty-one 11" x 11" squares from both top fabric and batiste.

2. Transfer the star design (page 111) onto the batiste with pencil. Permanent marker will show through the light-colored quilt top.

3. Pin the batiste and top fabric blocks together to avoid design shifting.

4. From the batiste side, hand or machine stitch channels created by the design.

5. Using a large-eye yarn needle, and again working from the wrong side of the block, thread the white 4-ply acrylic knitting worsted through the channels. Cut the yarn at the end of the run. A double strand of yarn normally fills the channel without puckering the work. If overstuffed, thread only a single strand of yarn through the star design.

6. Make twenty-one trapunto blocks in this manner.

7. Trim fifteen of the trapunto blocks to 10" x 10". These will be the center squares in the A units.

8. Trim five of the trapunto blocks to 10⅜" x 10⅜". Then cut in half diagonally for use on quilt's outer edge. These will be the half-square trapunto blocks used in the B units.

Love conquers all.

—Virgil
Eclogues

9. Following the illustration below for special cutting instructions for the last trapunto block, first cut the block in half diagonally. Then trim away ⅝" on the two short sides of one triangle (half-square triangle used in B unit). Trim away ¼" on the two short sides of the other triangle. Cut this triangle in half (two quarter-square triangles used in C units).

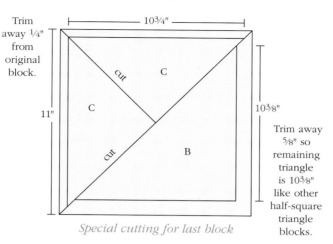

Special cutting for last block

Ocean Waves Units
2,268 triangles are required for this full-size quilt

10. Press and fold your fabrics. Stack three or four fabrics and cut 3⅛"-wide strips through all layers across the width of the fabric using a rotary cutter, ruler, and mat.

11. Then cut the strips into 3⅛" squares. Cut each square diagonally to form two triangles.

Ocean Waves Block Assembly
Described is one unit. You will need to make 84 total.

Each unit is made up of 12 light and 15 darker neutrals.

12. Make nine squares by sewing together light and darker triangles along the bias edge with an accurate ¼" seam allowance. Press seam toward the darker fabric.

13. Arrange your nine squares and additional triangles in sequence shown below. Notice that the lighter triangles are all turned the same direction.

14. Follow the illustration below for the piecing sequence. Finger press and pin seams to turn in opposite directions.

15. Sew into rows, then join rows to form ocean waves frame unit.

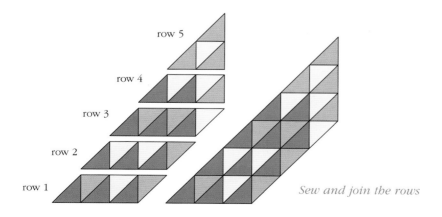

row 5
row 4
row 3
row 2
row 1

Sew and join the rows

Joining Ocean Waves Frames to Trapunto Blocks

CENTER SQUARE, A UNIT

16. Mark the point of seamline intersection (1/4" in from cut edges) on each ocean waves frame and trapunto block.

17. Sew each "frame" to the center trapunto square, starting and stopping the stitching at the mark you made, thus leaving seam allowances free.

18. Join the four mitered seams of the frame units by pinning the seam intersections and sewing from the outer edge in toward the center trapunto block stopping at the mark, being careful not to catch seam allowances in the seam. Press the mitered seams open.

19. Join fifteen square trapunto blocks with their ocean wave frame units, forming fifteen A units.

A unit

OUTER TRAPUNTO HALF-SQUARE TRAPUNTO BLOCKS, B UNITS

20. Join two ocean wave frames to each of the eleven half-square trapunto triangles following the illustration below.

CORNER QUARTER-SQUARE TRAPUNTO BLOCKS, C UNITS

21. Join each of the two quarter-square trapunto triangles to an ocean wave frame unit following the illustration below.

B unit

C unit

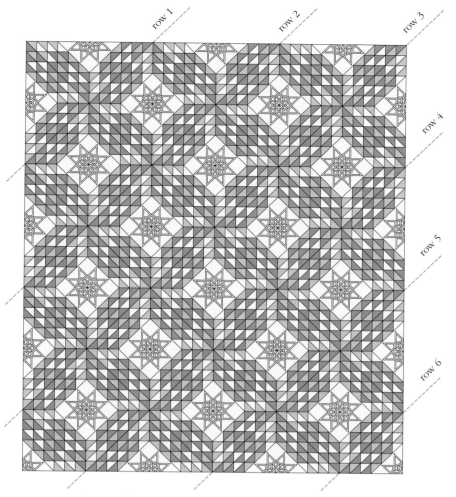

row 1 row 2 row 3 row 4 row 5 row 6

Block arrangement in diagonal set

QUILT ASSEMBLY

22. Pin the blocks together matching intersections and sew diagonal rows following the illustration above. Press seams open.

23. Stay stitch ⅛" from the outside edges of the quilt to prevent the bias edges from stretching.

24. Finally, join these six rows to see your finished quilt top!

LAYERING

25. Cut the 7½ yards of backing fabric into three 2½-yard lengths. Remove the selvage and use a ½" seam allowance to sew the three lengths together. Press the backing seams open. After measuring the quilt top, trim the backing so it is about 3" larger than the quilt top on all four sides.

26. Layer the backing (wrong side up), the batting, and the quilt top (right side up). Refer to page 81 for more detailed instructions.

QUILTING

Though large, this quilt can be nicely machine quilted. If you feel you've invested enough care with handwork in the trapunto blocks to warrant hand quilting them, you might still machine quilt the ocean waves. In deciding upon a quilting design plan, don't overlook the trapunto block. Though it looks fancy and complete with its raised star, remember this 9½" block must have additional stitching to secure it to the other quilt layers. Minimally, I recommend you intersect the block with quilting lines as illustrated below. But of course, any additional quilting you choose to do will only make your wedding gift more dear.

Quilting lines for trapunto blocks

BINDING

27. Cut nine strips of binding fabric 2¼" by the width of the fabric. Sew them together into one long strip. Fold the entire length of the strip in half lengthwise and press. Attach the raw edge to the quilt and finish sewing the binding by hand onto the back of the quilt. Refer to page 23 for more detailed instructions.

*While rivers run into the sea,
while on the mountains shadows
move over the slopes, while heaven
feeds the stars, ever shall thy
honor, thy name, and
thy praises endure.*

—Virgil
Eclogues

Trapunto Star
Pattern
(half of design)

Basic Techniques

Simple techniques can transform ribbons into heirloom projects with elegant textured details.

Making a Floral Bow

1. Hold the ribbon right side up between your thumb and index finger. Pinch the ribbon approximately 12" (or determined streamer length in project) from the end and then form a loop as large as you need, rolling the ribbon up and toward you. Place the long end of the ribbon between your thumb and index finger to form the bow's center.

Form the first loop.

2. Before forming the bottom loop, make a half twist to the left so the ribbon will be right side out, then roll the ribbon down and toward you. Pinch the ribbon together at the bow's center.

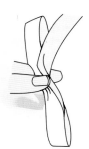

Form the next loop.

3. Continue forming loops until you have enough, keeping the loops the same size. Remember to always pinch the ribbon at the center and to always twist to the left before forming each loop.

4. Once the loops are completed, cut the end of the ribbon, leaving a streamer as long as required. Wrap and twist a 6" length of floral wire around the center of the bow to secure the loops.

Continue forming loops and secure with floral wire

Crazy Patch Block

1. Cut small angular pieces (at least 3½" on one side) of assorted fabrics for piecing.

2. Pin one fabric piece right side up in the center of the muslin backing specified in project instructions. Matching right sides and one raw edge of each piece, pin a second fabric piece over first piece. Sew a ¼" seam along matched edges; trim seam to ⅛" to eliminate bulk. Flip and press the second fabric piece over the seam allowances. Trim away excess fabric if necessary.

3. Working clockwise around the center fabric piece, sew another fabric piece to the next adjacent side of the center piece, covering the raw edges of the previously sewn piece. When you have gone completely around the center piece, trim the fabrics to create new angles.

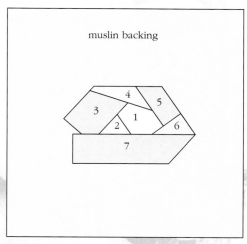

Crazy Patch block

4. Continue sewing fabric pieces, covering the raw edges, trimming the excess fabric, and pressing each piece before adding the next until the block measures the desired size.

5. Follow the project instructions to embellish the block with assorted embroidery stitches, silk ribbon embroidery, buttons, and/or beads.

Tea Dyeing

You may choose to age your project for various reasons—to hide an existing stain, or to make new fabrics, ribbons, and laces look old. Begin by testing the depth of stain desired. Dyeing a sample piece before trying the actual project may be a good idea, especially when working with sentimental items. Depending upon the size of the project, vary the amount of tea, water, and soaking time. Generally, begin by steeping a tea bag in two cups of hot water and allowing tea to cool. Soak the fabric or lace piece in tea several minutes or until desired stain is reached. Remove the item from the tea, rinse (optional), dry, and press. Rinsing before drying and pressing the project results in a lighter dye effect.

Embroidery

HERRINGBONE STITCH

Working from left to right, bring needle up at A and through fabric at B and out again at C (forming a horizontal straight stitch on wrong side of fabric). Continue working from the top to the bottom edge of the stitch.

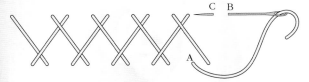

Herringbone stitch

LAZY DAISY STITCH

Use floss or perle cotton and follow Silk Ribbon Embroidery: Lazy Daisy Stitch (page 117).

FLY STITCH

Bring the needle out at A, loop down, and insert the needle at B, bringing the tip of the needle out over the top at C. Pull tight. Insert the needle through the fabric the desired length below C, forming a Y at D.

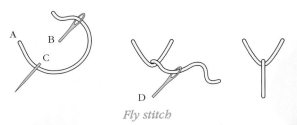

Fly stitch

FEATHER STITCH

Bring the needle through the fabric at A. Make a downward loop of ribbon or thread and insert the needle at B, bringing the tip of the needle out at C over the loop. Pull through. Continue the next stitch in the same manner, but insert the needle to the left approximately even with C. The loop should be on the left side. Bring the point of the needle out over the loop and pull through. Alternate to the right and left.

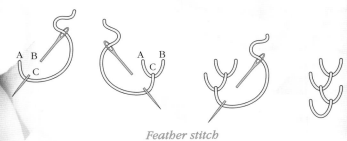

Feather stitch

BUTTONHOLE STITCH

Bring the needle through the fabric at A. Hold the thread down. Insert the needle at B and back up at C, bringing the needle over the thread. Pull into place and continue with B and C down the line. (Often used on edge of fabric.)

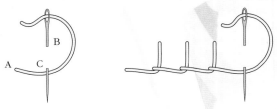

Buttonhole stitch

CHEVRON STITCH

Bring the needle up at A and down at B. Bring the needle up at D. Keeping the floss above the needle, insert at C and out again close to B. Complete the stitch by inserting the needle at E, and repeat the steps.

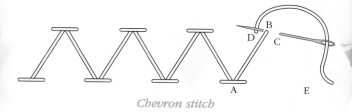

Chevron stitch

STEM STITCH

This stitch is generally worked in perle cotton or embroidery floss. Always work from left to right, keeping your thread below the needle. Draw a line in the desired position. Bring the needle up from the back of the fabric at A. Hold the thread beneath the thumb, go down at B, and up at C. Continue going down a short distance to the right of the stitching line and coming up right next to the previous stitch.

Stem stitch

FRENCH KNOT

Use floss and follow Silk Ribbon Embroidery: French Knot (page 117).

Silk Ribbon Embroidery

Use a chenille needle (#22 or #20 for 2mm or 4mm ribbon, #18 for 7mm and larger ribbon). Cut silk ribbon approximately 12" to 14" long.

NEEDLE EYE LOCK

To thread the ribbon, place the ribbon through the eye of the needle and pierce this end of the ribbon approximately ¼" from the end with the point of the needle. Push the ribbon down half the length of the needle, and

holding the tip of the needle, pull on the ribbon from the long end until the ribbon locks at the eye of the needle.

Lock ribbon at eye of needle.

KNOT THE END

Insert the needle in the end of the ribbon and take a small stitch going in toward the ribbon from the cut end. Pull the needle through the ribbon and push the stitch down the length of the needle and ribbon, leaving a small loop at the end.

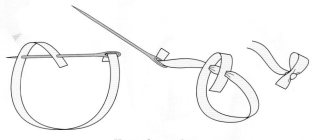

Knot the end.

INTERLOCK

When adding to previous ribbon, pull to the back side and cut a ¾" tail. Thread new ribbon and knot as before. Pierce through the ¾" tail of previous ribbon close to the fabric and pull new ribbon through until the knot catches. Continue with stitches.

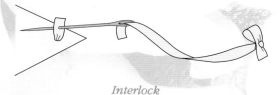

Interlock

KNOTTING TO END DESIGN

When finished with an area, take the needle to the wrong side of fabric. Run the needle under a few stitches or hold a ribbon from another stitch tightly to the wrong side of the fabric while piercing through it with the needle. Pull gently through pierced ribbon and take another stitch through the same ribbon. Pull tighter the second time.

SPIDER WEB ROSE

1. Imagine a circle like a clock. Using perle cotton to match ribbon for the rose, bring the needle through the fabric at eleven o'clock. Hold the thread loosely, making a downward loop. Go down at one o'clock and up in the center of the imaginary circle. Pass the needle over the downward looped thread and go down at six o'clock, forming a Y. This is the fly stitch.

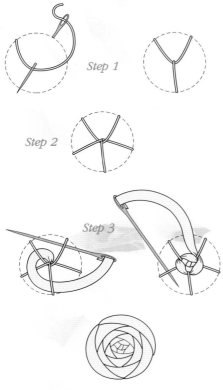

Spider web rose

2. To make spokes for the spider web rose, bring the needle up just before nine o'clock. Go down in the center. Bring the needle up just after three o'clock. Go down in the center. Knot on the back and cut.

3. Use silk ribbon and come up in the center of the spokes and begin weaving over one spoke, under the next, and pull in toward the center, repeat over, under, pull in. Continue in this manner, pulling fairly tight at center, then leaving the ribbon looser as you work out. The key to a pretty rose is to twist the ribbon and keep it loose, especially as you near the outer edge. Weave until the spokes are covered, then bring the needle around the last spoke and go down through the fabric and knot.

RUCHED ROSE

Cut a 14" length of ribbon. Measure and mark ¾" distances with pins along the ribbon. Use matching thread and stitch a zigzag gathering line along the ribbon. Gently pull up the gathers until it is nicely ruffled. Spread the gathers evenly. Curve the ribbon around so the inner scallops touch. Placing the ruching on the project, tack the scallops together using matching thread. Spiral the ruching counterclockwise so the second layer is behind the first.

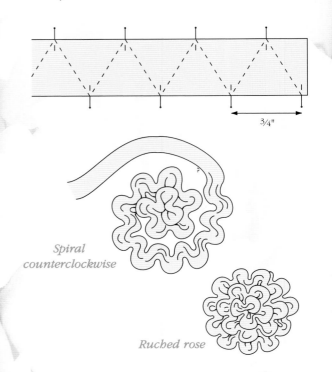

Spiral counterclockwise

Ruched rose

JAPANESE RIBBON STITCH

1. Come up at A, flatten the ribbon, and stitch down through the center of the ribbon at B.

2. Pull the ribbon gently so the ribbon edges begin to curl at the point. There are two choices for finishing this stitch. For a squared end, pull the ribbon only to the point where it starts to curl. For a pointed end, slowly pull the ribbon further until the sides start to roll inward at the tip. (Be careful not to pull too tightly or the effect is lost.)

Japanese ribbon stitch (squared end)

Japanese ribbon stitch (pointed end)

LAZY DAISY STITCH

1. Bring the needle up at A. Make a loop with the ribbon and go down through the fabric at B, next to A (being careful not to pierce the ribbon at A). Before taking the needle completely through fabric, bring the point of the needle up at C (with needle going over the looped ribbon).

2. Pull the ribbon through. Anchor the stitch by going down at D.

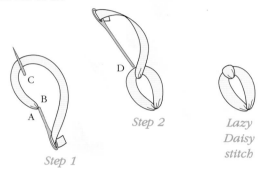

Step 1   Step 2   Lazy Daisy stitch

LOOP STITCH

1. Bring the needle through the fabric at A. Lay ribbon flat and loop up and over, piercing the fabric at B (directly above beginning of stitch).

2. Begin to pull ribbon through slowly over your finger, keeping it from twisting. When the desired size is reached, hold the loop with the thumb while you start the next loop. Continue making loops, always holding the previous loops so they don't pull out as you pull on the ribbon for the new loop. For a flower, work each loop around a center point. Work French or colonial knot(s), or sew a pearl or bead in the center to complete the flower.

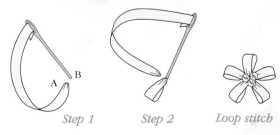

Step 1   Step 2   Loop stitch

STEM STITCH

Use ribbon and follow Embroidery: Stem Stitch (page 115).

FRENCH KNOT

1. Bring the needle up through the fabric. Lay the needle on top of the ribbon close to where it came through the fabric; wrap the ribbon up and over the point of the needle (wrap around the needle twice for a normal knot, wrap once for a smaller knot, and three times or more for a larger knot).

2. Hold the ribbon securely to one side as you insert the needle into the fabric next to the starting point. Pull the needle through the fabric.

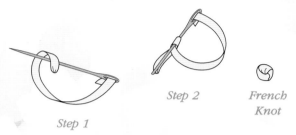

Step 1   Step 2   French Knot

CORAL STITCH

Come up at A. Lay the ribbon along the intended stitching line. Bring the needle down at B, and up at C, with the loop below point of the needle.

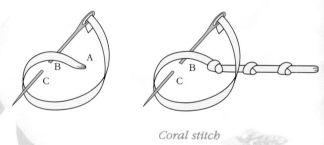

Coral stitch

COUCHING

1. Make a long stitch along the desired stitching line.

2. Come back up at A and stitch over the ribbon, going down at B. Continue along the length of the first stitch.

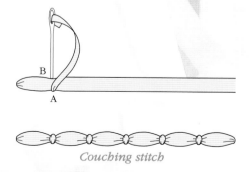

Couching stitch

FRENCH KNOT COUCHING

For a variation, use French knots instead of stitching over the ribbon to create the couching.

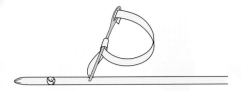

French knot couching

FRENCH KNOT COUCHED BOW

1. To make a couched bow, thread the needle with the desired length of ribbon without locking the ribbon on the needle. Take a small stitch at the position of the bow. Pull the ribbon halfway through the fabric, leaving equal lengths of ribbon at each side of the stitch; remove the needle. Tie the ribbon into a bow.

2. Shape the bow by twisting the ribbon and securing the loops and streamers with French knots or couching over the ribbon.

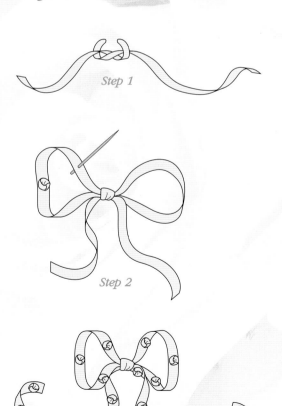

Step 1

Step 2

French knot couched ribbon bow

Making Ribbon Flowers and Leaves

Note: If desired, use small pieces of crinoline as a base to sew and construct each flower or leaf. This is especially helpful for the large petal and crushed roses.

LOOP PETAL FLOWER

1. Refer to the illustration below and loop the wired ribbon to create six to seven approximately 2"-wide loops (smaller loops will make a smaller flower).

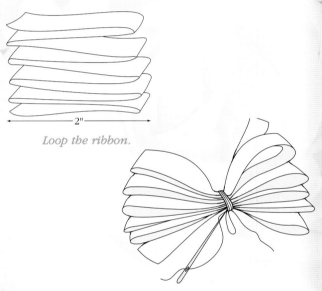

Loop the ribbon.

Stitch at center edges and knot.

Loop Petal flower

2. Use a threaded needle to take a stitch at the center edges of the layered ribbon; tightly wrap the ribbon center with thread; knot and trim the thread. Separate the loops and begin to crush and crimp the loops to create the flower. Sew several stamens to the center if desired.

CRUSHED ROSE

(Note: For a rosebud, use a 12" length of ribbon.)

1. Fold one end of a 36" length of ribbon under ⅛" twice.

Fold end under.

2. Gently pull the wire from the end opposite the folds to gather the ribbon.

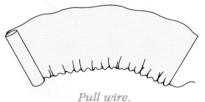

Pull wire.

3. Wrap the end of the ribbon with the excess wire, a couple of times; cut off the excess wire.

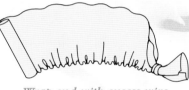

Wrap end with excess wire.

4. Roll the rose from the wrapped end, using matching thread to hand sew the gathered ribbon edge to itself.

5. Crush the rose in your hands to give it a dried rose look, and smash it flat between your palms. Push the rolls to one side so the gathers, stitches, and folded end are hidden.

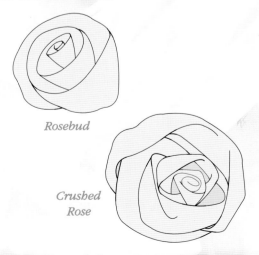

Rosebud

Crushed Rose

PRIMROSE

Pull the wire ends or use a running stitch to gather a 6" length of ribbon along one long edge to form a U shape (Step 1). With right sides together, sew the ends of the ribbon together (Step 2). Gently pull the wire or thread to form a tight center. If desired, place five or six stamens in the center of the primrose before securing the center gathers.

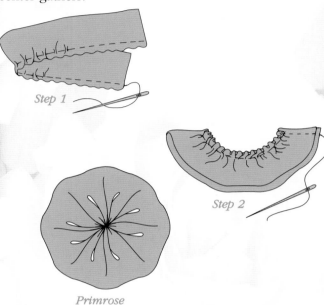

Step 1

Step 2

Primrose

HALF PRIMROSE

Refer to the primrose instructions above to make half primrose in the same manner using a 4½" length of ribbon, securing the gathers at each end (Steps 1 and 2). Do not join to form a circle.

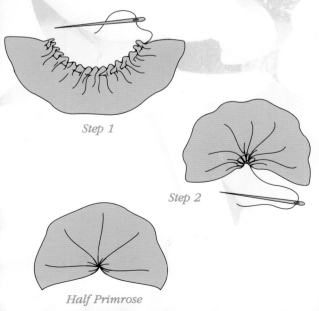

Step 1

Step 2

Half Primrose

FLOWER WITH FIVE OR THREE PETALS

For a flower with five petals, leave about ⅛" at each end and fold a 12" length of wired ribbon (for smaller-petal flower use a 10" length of ribbon) into five equal sections. (For ribbon without wired edges, mark each section with a pencil mark at the edge.) Remove the wire from the lower edge of the ribbon. Beginning with a knotted thread, use a short running stitch to stitch the petal sections within each divided ribbon section.

Gently pull the thread to form the petals; knot to secure the gathered petals. If desired, sew stamens to the center of the flower. Overlap the petals at the ends to form the flower; stitch to secure. For a beaded center, sew or glue seed beads to the center of the flower.

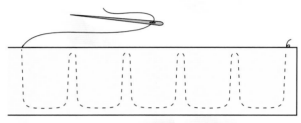

Stitch petal sections.

Flower with five petals

For the flower with three petals, see the illustration below and follow the stitching and gathering instructions of flower with five petals to divide a 7" length of ribbon into three equal sections. Secure the gathered petals.

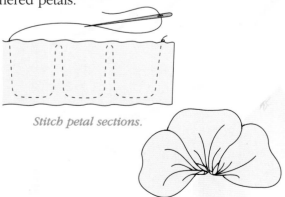

Stitch petal sections.

Flower with three petals

LARGE RUFFLED-PETAL FLOWER

1. Cut four 9" lengths of 1½"-wide wired ribbon. Gently pull the wire at the lower edge of one ribbon length and gather as tight as possible. (For ribbon without wired edges, simply use a running stitch to gather the edge.) Pull the wire to the back of the flower, twist the ends together, and tuck them behind the petal. Starting at one end of the petal and about ⅛" from the top of the petal, make a knot, then take small stitches across the ribbon.

Pull lower wire, stitch top edge.

2. Gently pull the thread to gather the petal until the desired look is achieved. Repeat to make three more petals.

3. Inserting stamens under the top petal, overlap the petals to form the flower and stitch together.

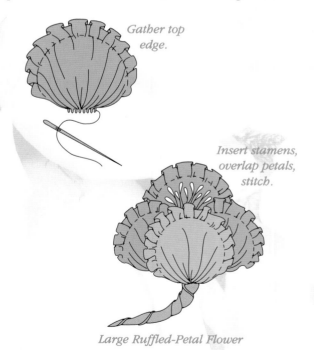

Gather top edge.

Insert stamens, overlap petals, stitch.

Large Ruffled-Petal Flower

FUCHSIA

Cut a 3½" length from 1½"-wide ribbon. Fold the ribbon ends to the center. Whip stitch three stamens to the center of the ribbon. Use a running stitch to stitch a diamond shape, with each point of the diamond at the center edges of ribbon. Pull the thread to form the petals of the flower. Backstitch and knot the thread to secure the petals.

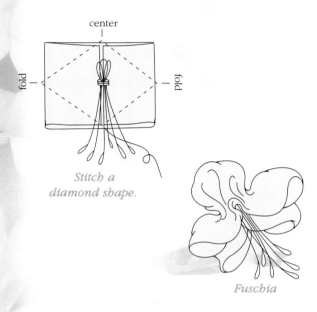

Stitch a diamond shape.

Fuschia

FUCHSIA WITH CENTER BUD

1. Using a 3" length of 1"-wide ribbon, stitch stamens to the center edge of the ribbon. Trim the stamens.

2. Fold the ends of the ribbon to the center, overlapping at an angle, and stitch to gather the edge of the bud; knot to secure.

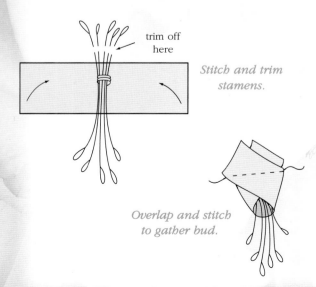

Stitch and trim stamens.

Overlap and stitch to gather bud.

3. Cut a 3½" length of 1½"-wide ribbon. Fold ribbon ends to center. Sew bud with stamens to lower edge of folded ribbon. Use a running stitch to stitch a diamond shape, with each point of diamond at center edges of ribbon. Pull thread to form petals of flower. Backstitch and knot thread to secure petals.

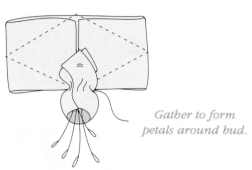

Gather to form petals around bud.

Fuschia with Center Bud

STEM

Use desired length of wired ribbon and twist the ribbon around itself to form the stem. The wire edges will help to keep the stem firm and will make it easy to shape and bend. Take a stitch at each end of the ribbon stem to secure the twists.

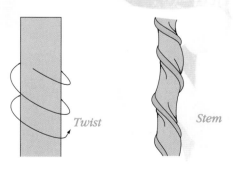

Twist

Stem

STEM AND CALYX

1. Fold an 8" length of wired ribbon twice diagonally (folds should be closer to one end of the ribbon than the other).

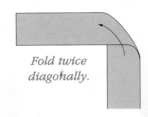

Fold twice diagonally.

2. Fold a small tuck in the center part of the calyx.

3. Firmly hold the ribbon at the tuck and twist the ends of the ribbon together to form the stem.

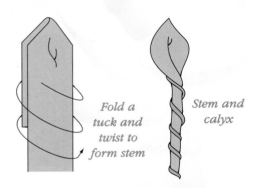

Fold a tuck and twist to form stem

Stem and calyx

FOLDED LEAF

1. Fold a 2½" length of ribbon twice diagonally.

2. Fold a small tuck in the center of folded ribbon.

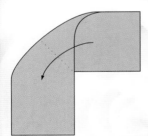

Fold twice diagonally.

Fold a small tuck.

3. Stitch across lower edge to gather and secure.

Gather and secure.

Folded leaf

GATHERED LEAF

1. Meet ends of a 7" length of ribbon together with right side of ribbon to inside.

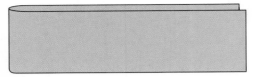

Fold ribbon.

2. Fold the corners of the ribbon.

Fold corners

3. Turn the ribbon over and use a running stitch along the first diagonal and take one backstitch three-quarters of the way. Continue the running stitch along the edges of the ribbon.

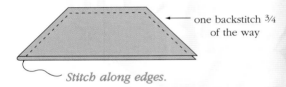

one backstitch ¾ of the way

Stitch along edges.

4. Pull the thread to gather the leaf; secure the gathers and open the leaf.

Gathered leaf

Postscript

Thank you for allowing us to share the very personal and memorable aspects of our wedding. Most of all we want you to develop ideas that mirror your own interests to make your wedding special and unique. We realize that some of the projects take time, but we feel the instructions are clear to even the novice. Finally, gifts that are handmade are also heart made. Your family and friends will share your happiness and love and forever remember this as one of life's eventful moments.

Sources

The Cotton Patch Mail Order
3405 Hall Lane, Dept. CTB
Lafayette, CA 94549
e-mail: cottonpa@aol.com
(800) 835-4418
(510) 283-7883
Retail quilting supplies

Ruth Cox
6901 Southeast 14th #160
Des Moines, IA 50320
(515) 287-7835
One-of-a-kind soft sculpture dolls

Donna's Country Collection
234 5th Street
West Des Moines, IA 50265
(515 274-2522
Retail quilting and silk ribbon embroidery supplies, teddy bear making patterns and supplies

Gooseberry Hill
1881 Old Lincoln Highway
Coalville, UT 84017
(801) 336-2780
Retail and wholesale patterns for clothing, teddy bears and ribbonwork; videos on bearmaking and ribbonwork; french ribbons, lace gloves, and collars

Indygo Junction, Inc.
P.O. Box 30238
Kansas City, MO 64112
(913) 341- 5559
(913) 341-7913 fax
Retail and wholesale patterns and books for wearables, dolls, and quilting

Quilters' Resource, Inc.
P.O. Box 148850
Chicago, IL 60614
(800) 676-6543
(312) 278-5695 fax
Wholesale silk and wire edged Elegance Ribbons®, trims, antique buttons, embellishments and books

Acknowledgments

Putting this book together has been a wonderful experience thanks to talented, creative people who have contributed to the project.

To the designers, with their individual talents, thank you for your unique ideas and the time and effort you committed to this publication.

Patrick Lose and Lenny Houts are two shining stars who designed and made the most beautiful wedding gown, which was a perfect reflection of my interests. As "Out On a Whim" Pat and Lenny are well known for their many licensed products, fabrics, dolls, and illustrations. I feel most fortunate to have benefited from their talents at both a personal and professional level.

Ruth Cox is a self-taught doll artist who makes whimsical dolls that range from six to sixty inches tall. Her "Hat Lady" dolls are always decked out in clothes made from vintage or recycled house dresses, lace curtains, and frequently she uses shoes which have a "goodwill" sticker.

Sandy Belt has many talents, from designing clothing and unique accessories, to creating one-of-a-kind dolls and animals. Her artistic flair with vintage pieces is evident in the many Victorian wedding accents she contributed to this book.

Donna Martin is first of all "Mom," and as the real mother of the bride, her interest in this book was rather significant. One might give her the "lifetime achievement award" for her part. I know she enjoyed every minute and is really the one who gave me that extra push. Crafting, quilting, and stitching have always been her passion, and her talents are reflected in the many projects she dedicated to this book. But most of all she is a great mom and best friend.

Ninette Gehle's passion for creating with fabrics was encouraged throughout her upbringing in Belgium. I found Ninette's work at a wonderful little shop called Eclectics in Kansas City. These creations from vintage fabrics and laces are one-of-a-kind with exquisite embellishments of pearls and crystals.

June Wildash Decker is our infamous Australian designer who lives in Iowa. She began doing "fancy work" as a very young child and is a very creative designer. She can transform silk ribbons into glorious arrangements of flowers on garments or accessories.

Carolie A. Hensley, Marg Gair, Ann Boyce, Nicki Jean, and Wendy McGrath are the talented designers that created and shared the beautiful heirloom quilts.

A special thanks also goes to those involved in the production of this publication.

Thanks to our photographers, Tracy Thompson, Gary Rhoman, and Sharon Risedorph for their patience and attention to detail.

Thanks to photo stylist Kayte Price, who provided endless ideas and creative approaches, resulting in the artistic and beautiful photographs throughout this publication.

Our technical writer and designer, Margaret Cox, did an excellent job assisting me in the organization, writing, and editing of this book. Without Margaret this book would still be only a dream for my mother and me. Also, appreciation is extended to the staff at C&T Publishing for their commitment from the very beginning to publish this extra-special book.

Index